Horse Racing Diary 2017

PERSONAL DETAILS

NAME

ADDRESS

TELEPHONE NUMBER

NHS NO

BLOOD GROUP

PASSPORT NO.

DRIVING LICENSE NO.

Handy Permutation Chart

No Of Selections	Doubles	Trebles	4 Folds	5 Folds	6 Folds	7 Folds	8 Folds	9 Folds	10 Folds
1									
2	1								
3	3	1							
4	6	4	1						
5	10	10	5	1					
6	15	20	15	6	1				
7	21	35	35	21	7	1			
8	28	56	70	56	28	8	1		
9	36	84	126	126	84	36	9	1	
10	45	120	210	252	210	120	45	10	1

Sunday	Catterick Bridge	Jump	Turf	Afternoon
01 January 2017	Cheltenham	Jump	Turf	Afternoon
	Exeter	Jump	Turf	Afternoon
	Fakenham	Jump	Turf	Afternoon
	Musselburgh	Jump	Turf	Afternoon
	Southwell	Flat	AW	Afternoon

Notes

THE FAIRLAWNE HANDICAP STEEPLE CHASE (CLASS 1)

THE DIPPER NOVICES' STEEPLE CHASE (CLASS 1)

THE OSBORNE HOUSE RELKEEL HURDLE RACE (CLASS 1)

Monday	Ayr	Jump	Turf	Afternoon
02 January 2017	Plumpton	Jump	Turf	Afternoon
	Southwell	Flat	AW	Afternoon

Notes

New Year's Day (Substitute day)

Tuesday	Bangor-On-Dee	Jump	Turf	Afternoon
03 January 2017	Musselburgh	Jump	Turf	Afternoon
	Newcastle	Flat	AW	Afternoon

Notes

Wednesday	Hereford	Jump	Turf	Afternoon
04 January 2017	Lingfield Park	Flat	AW	Afternoon
	Newcastle	Flat	AW	Afternoon
	Wolves	Flat	AW	Twilight

Notes

Thursday	Chelmsford City	Flat	AW	Evening
05 January 2017	Lingfield Park	Jump	Turf	Afternoon
	Southwell	Flat	AW	Afternoon
	Wolves	Flat	AW	Afternoon

Notes

Friday	Kempton Park	Flat	AW	Afternoon
06 January 2017	Ludlow	Jump	Turf	Afternoon
	Wetherby	Jump	Turf	Afternoon
	Wolves	Flat	AW	Evening

Notes

Saturday	Lingfield Park	Flat	AW	Afternoon
07 January 2017	Newcastle	Jump	Turf	Afternoon
	Sandown Park	Jump	Turf	Afternoon
	Wincanton	Jump	Turf	Afternoon
	Wolves	Flat	AW	Evening

Notes

THE 32Red TOLWORTH HURDLE RACE (A NOVICES' HURDLE RACE)

Sunday	Chepstow	Jump	Turf	Afternoon
08 January 2017	Fontwell Park	Jump	Turf	Afternoon

Notes

Monday	Doncaster	Jump	Turf	Afternoon
09 January 2017	Lingfield Park	Flat	AW	Afternoon
	Wolves	Flat	AW	Afternoon

Notes

Tuesday	Lingfield Park	Jump	Turf	Afternoon
10 January 2017	Southwell	Flat	AW	Afternoon
	Wolves	Flat	AW	Afternoon

Notes

Wednesday	Hereford	Jump	Turf	Afternoon
11 January 2017	Kempton Park	Flat	AW	Twilight
	Newcastle	Flat	AW	Afternoon
	Taunton	Jump	Turf	Afternoon

Notes

Thursday 12 January 2017	Catterick Bridge	Jump	Turf	Afternoon
	Chelmsford City	Flat	AW	Evening
	Leicester	Jump	Turf	Afternoon
	Newcastle	Flat	AW	Afternoon

Notes

Friday 13 January 2017	Huntingdon	Jump	Turf	Afternoon
	Lingfield Park	Flat	AW	Afternoon
	Sedgefield	Jump	Turf	Afternoon
	Wolves	Flat	AW	Evening

Notes

11

Saturday	Kempton Park	Jump	Turf	Afternoon
14 January 2017	Lingfield Park	Flat	AW	Afternoon
	Warwick	Jump	Turf	Afternoon
	Wetherby	Jump	Turf	Afternoon
	Wolves	Flat	AW	Evening

Notes

THE BETFRED CLASSIC STEEPLE CHASE (A HANDICAP)

THE NEPTUNE INVESTMENT MANAGEMENT NOVICES'
HURDLE RACE (CLASS 1)

| **Sunday** | Fakenham | Jump | Turf | Afternoon |
| **15 January 2017** | Kelso | Jump | Turf | Afternoon |

Notes

Monday	Ayr	Jump	Turf	Afternoon
16 January 2017	Plumpton	Jump	Turf	Afternoon
	Wolves	Flat	AW	Afternoon

Notes

Tuesday

17 January 2017

Ayr	Jump	Turf	Afternoon
Exeter	Jump	Turf	Afternoon
Kempton Park	Flat	AW	Afternoon

Notes

Wednesday

18 January 2017

Kempton Park	Flat	AW	Twilight
Lingfield Park	Flat	AW	Afternoon
Market Rasen	Jump	Turf	Afternoon
Newbury	Jump	Turf	Afternoon

Notes

14

Thursday	Chelmsford City	Flat	AW	Evening
19 January 2017	Ludlow	Jump	Turf	Afternoon
	Southwell	Flat	AW	Afternoon
	Wincanton	Jump	Turf	Afternoon

Notes

Friday	Chepstow	Jump	Turf	Afternoon
20 January 2017	Lingfield Park	Flat	AW	Afternoon
	Musselburgh	Jump	Turf	Afternoon
	Wolves	Flat	AW	Evening

Notes

Saturday	Ascot	Jump	Turf	Afternoon
21 January	Haydock Park	Jump	Turf	Afternoon
2017				
	Lingfield Park	Flat	AW	Afternoon
	Newcastle	Flat	AW	Evening
	Taunton	Jump	Turf	Afternoon

Notes

THE SODEXO CLARENCE HOUSE STEEPLE CHASE (CLASS 1)

THE KELTBRAY HOLLOWAY'S HURDLE RACE (A LIMITED HANDICAP)

THE OLBG.com MARES' HURDLE RACE (CLASS 1)

THE ALTCAR NOVICES' STEEPLE CHASE (CLASS 1)

THE PETER MARSH STEEPLE CHASE (A LIMITED HANDICAP)

THE StanJames.com CHAMPION HURDLE TRIAL (CLASS 1)

THE SKY BET SUPREME TRIAL NOVICES' HURDLE RACE (CLASS 1)

Sunday	Fontwell Park	Jump	Turf	Afternoon
22 January 2017	Hereford	Jump	Turf	Afternoon

Notes

Monday	Bangor-On-Dee	Jump	Turf	Afternoon
23 January 2017	Newcastle	Jump	Turf	Afternoon
	Wolves	Flat	AW	Afternoon

Notes

17

Tuesday	Leicester	Jump	Turf	Afternoon
24 January 2017	Southwell	Flat	AW	Afternoon
	Wetherby	Jump	Turf	Afternoon

Notes

Wednesday	Catterick Bridge	Jump	Turf	Afternoon
25 January 2017	Lingfield Park	Flat	AW	Afternoon
	Ludlow	Jump	Turf	Afternoon
	Newcastle	Flat	AW	Twilight

Notes

Thursday	Fakenham	Jump	Turf	Afternoon
26 January 2017	Southwell	Flat	AW	Afternoon
	Warwick	Jump	Turf	Afternoon
	Wolves	Flat	AW	Evening

Notes

Friday	Doncaster	Jump	Turf	Afternoon
27 January 2017	Huntingdon	Jump	Turf	Afternoon
	Lingfield Park	Flat	AW	Afternoon
	Newcastle	Flat	AW	Evening

Notes

Saturday	Cheltenham	Jump	Turf	Afternoon
28 January 2017	Doncaster	Jump	Turf	Afternoon
	Kempton Park	Flat	AW	Evening
	Lingfield Park	Flat	AW	Afternoon
	Uttoxeter	Jump	Turf	Afternoon

Notes

THE freebets.com TROPHY STEEPLE CHASE (A HANDICAP) (CLASS 1)

THE galliardhomes.com CLEEVE HURDLE RACE (CLASS 1)

THE JCB TRIUMPH HURDLE TRIAL (A JUVENILE HURDLE RACE) (CLASS 1)

THE COTSWOLD STEEPLE CHASE (CLASS 1)

THE NEPTUNE INVESTMENT MANAGEMENT NOVICES' HURDLE RACE (CLASS 1)

THE LIGHTNING NOVICES' STEEPLE CHASE (CLASS 1)

THE RIVER DON NOVICES' HURDLE RACE (CLASS 1)

THE OLBG.com MARES' HURDLE RACE (CLASS 1)

Sunday	Fontwell Park	Jump	Turf	Afternoon
29 January 2017	Sedgefield	Jump	Turf	Afternoon

Notes

Monday	Ayr	Jump	Turf	Afternoon
30 January 2017	Plumpton	Jump	Turf	Afternoon
	Southwell	Flat	AW	Afternoon

Notes

Tuesday	Lingfield Park	Jump	Turf	Afternoon
31 January	Southwell	Jump	Turf	Afternoon
2017	Wolves	Flat	AW	Afternoon

Notes

Wednesday	Hereford	Jump	Turf	Afternoon
01	Kempton Park	Flat	AW	Afternoon
February	Leicester	Jump	Turf	Afternoon
2017	Newcastle	Flat	AW	Twilight

Notes

Thursday 02 February 2017	Chelmsford City	Flat	AW	Evening
	Southwell	Flat	AW	Afternoon
	Towcester	Jump	Turf	Afternoon
	Wincanton	Jump	Turf	Afternoon

Notes

Friday 03 February 2017	Catterick Bridge	Jump	Turf	Afternoon
	Chepstow	Jump	Turf	Afternoon
	Kempton Park	Flat	AW	Evening
	Lingfield Park	Flat	AW	Afternoon

Notes

Saturday	Lingfield Park	Flat	AW	Afternoon
04	Musselburgh	Jump	Turf	Afternoon
February				
2017				
	Newcastle	Flat	AW	Evening
	Sandown Park	Jump	Turf	Afternoon
	Wetherby	Jump	Turf	Afternoon

Notes

THE BETFRED MOBILE AND LEVY BOARD HEROES
HANDICAP HURDLE RACE
THE BETFRED TV SCILLY ISLES NOVICES' STEEPLE CHASE
(CLASS 1)
THE totepool TOWTON NOVICES' STEEPLE CHASE (CLASS 1)

24

Sunday	Musselburgh	Jump	Turf	Afternoon
05 February 2017	Taunton	Jump	Turf	Afternoon
	Notes			

Monday	Lingfield Park	Jump	Turf	Afternoon
06 February 2017	Sedgefield	Jump	Turf	Afternoon
	Wolves	Flat	AW	Afternoon
	Notes			

Tuesday	Hereford	Jump	Turf	Afternoon
07	Market Rasen	Jump	Turf	Afternoon
February				
2017				
	Newcastle	Flat	AW	Afternoon

Notes

Wednesday	Carlisle	Jump	Turf	Afternoon
08	Chelmsford City	Flat	AW	Afternoon
February				
2017				
	Kempton Park	Flat	AW	Twilight
	Ludlow	Jump	Turf	Afternoon

Notes

Thursday 09 February 2017	Chelmsford City	Flat	AW	Evening
	Doncaster	Jump	Turf	Afternoon
	Huntingdon	Jump	Turf	Afternoon
	Lingfield Park	Flat	AW	Afternoon

Notes

Friday 10 February 2017	Bangor-On-Dee	Jump	Turf	Afternoon
	Kempton Park	Jump	Turf	Afternoon
	Newcastle	Flat	AW	Evening
	Southwell	Flat	AW	Afternoon

Notes

27

Saturday

11
February
2017

Lingfield Park	Flat	AW	Afternoon
Newbury	Jump	Turf	Afternoon
Uttoxeter	Jump	Turf	Afternoon
Warwick	Jump	Turf	Afternoon
Wolves	Flat	AW	Evening

Notes

THE BETFAIR HURDLE RACE (HANDICAP) (CLASS 1)
THE BETFAIR DENMAN STEEPLE CHASE (CLASS 1)
THE GAME SPIRIT STEEPLE CHASE (CLASS 1)
THE KINGMAKER NOVICES' STEEPLE CHASE (CLASS 1)

Sunday	Exeter	Jump	Turf	Afternoon
12	Sedgefield	Jump	Turf	Afternoon
February				
2017				

Notes

Monday	Catterick Bridge	Jump	Turf	Afternoon
13	Plumpton	Jump	Turf	Afternoon
February				
2017	Wolves	Flat	AW	Afternoon

Notes

29

Tuesday	Ayr	Jump	Turf	Afternoon
14	Fontwell Park	Jump	Turf	Afternoon
February				
2017				
	Newcastle	Flat	AW	Afternoon

Notes

Wednesday	Kempton Park	Flat	AW	Twilight
15	Newcastle	Jump	Turf	Afternoon
February				
2017				
	Towcester	Jump	Turf	Afternoon
	Wolves	Flat	AW	Afternoon

Notes

Thursday **16** **February** **2017**	Chelmsford City	Flat	AW	Evening
	Kelso	Jump	Turf	Afternoon
	Leicester	Jump	Turf	Afternoon
	Lingfield Park	Flat	AW	Afternoon

Notes

Friday **17** **February** **2017**	Fakenham	Jump	Turf	Afternoon
	Newcastle	Flat	AW	Afternoon
	Sandown Park	Jump	Turf	Afternoon
	Wolves	Flat	AW	Evening

Notes

THE JANE SEYMOUR MARES' NOVICES' HURDLE RACE
(CLASS 1)

Saturday	Ascot	Jump	Turf	Afternoon
18 **February** **2017**	Haydock Park	Jump	Turf	Afternoon
	Kempton Park	Flat	AW	Evening
	Lingfield Park	Flat	AW	Afternoon
	Wincanton	Jump	Turf	Afternoon

Notes

THE REYNOLDSTOWN NOVICES' STEEPLE CHASE (CLASS 1)

THE BETFAIR ASCOT STEEPLE CHASE (CLASS 1)

THE PRESTIGE NOVICES' HURDLE RACE (CLASS 1)

THE RENDLESHAM HURDLE RACE (CLASS 1)

THE BETFRED GRAND NATIONAL TRIAL (A HANDICAP STEEPLE CHASE)

THE BATHWICK TYRES KINGWELL HURDLE

| **Sunday** | Ffos Las | Jump | Turf | Afternoon |
| **19 February 2017** | Market Rasen | Jump | Turf | Afternoon |

Notes

Monday	Carlisle	Jump	Turf	Afternoon
20 February 2017	Lingfield Park	Jump	Turf	Afternoon
	Wolves	Flat	AW	Afternoon

Notes

Tuesday	Southwell	Flat	AW	Afternoon
21	Taunton	Jump	Turf	Afternoon
February				
2017	Wetherby	Jump	Turf	Afternoon

Notes

Wednesday	Doncaster	Jump	Turf	Afternoon
22	Kempton Park	Flat	AW	Twilight
February				
2017	Lingfield Park	Flat	AW	Afternoon
	Ludlow	Jump	Turf	Afternoon

Notes

Thursday 23 February 2017	Chelmsford City	Flat	AW	Afternoon
	Huntingdon	Jump	Turf	Afternoon
	Sedgefield	Jump	Turf	Afternoon
	Wolves	Flat	AW	Evening

Notes

Friday 24 February 2017	Exeter	Jump	Turf	Afternoon
	Lingfield Park	Flat	AW	Afternoon
	Warwick	Jump	Turf	Afternoon
	Wolves	Flat	AW	Evening

Notes

Saturday	Chepstow	Jump	Turf	Afternoon
25 **February** **2017**	Kempton Park	Jump	Turf	Afternoon
	Lingfield Park	Flat	AW	Afternoon
	Newcastle	Jump	Turf	Afternoon
	Wolves	Flat	AW	Evening

Notes

THE BetBright STEEPLE CHASE (HANDICAP) (CLASS 1)
THE BetBright ADONIS JUVENILE HURDLE RACE (CLASS 1)
THE BetBright PENDIL NOVICES' STEEPLE CHASE (CLASS 1)
THE SKY BET DOVECOTE NOVICES' HURDLE RACE (CLASS 1)
THE coral.co.uk WINTER DERBY (CLASS 1)

Sunday	Fontwell Park	Jump	Turf	Afternoon
26	Southwell	Jump	Turf	Afternoon
February				
2017				

Notes
THE totepool NATIONAL SPIRIT HURDLE RACE (CLASS 1)

Monday	Ayr	Jump	Turf	Afternoon
27	Plumpton	Jump	Turf	Afternoon
February				
2017	Wolves	Flat	AW	Afternoon

Notes

Tuesday	Catterick Bridge	Jump	Turf	Afternoon
28	Leicester	Jump	Turf	Afternoon
February				
2017	Lingfield Park	Flat	AW	Afternoon

Notes

Wednesday	Ffos Las	Jump	Turf	Afternoon
01 March	Musselburgh	Jump	Turf	Afternoon
2017	Newcastle	Flat	AW	Twilight
	Wincanton	Jump	Turf	Afternoon

Notes

Thursday	Chelmsford City	Flat	AW	Evening
02 March 2017	Ludlow	Jump	Turf	Afternoon
	Newcastle	Flat	AW	Afternoon
	Taunton	Jump	Turf	Afternoon

Notes

Friday	Doncaster	Jump	Turf	Afternoon
03 March 2017	Lingfield Park	Flat	AW	Afternoon
	Newbury	Jump	Turf	Afternoon
	Newcastle	Flat	AW	Evening

Notes

Saturday	Doncaster	Jump	Turf	Afternoon
04 March	Kelso	Jump	Turf	Afternoon
2017				
	Lingfield Park	Flat	AW	Afternoon
	Newbury	Jump	Turf	Afternoon
	Newcastle	Flat	AW	Evening

Notes

THE totescoop6 PREMIER KELSO HURDLE RACE (CLASS 1)

THE StanJames.com SUPPORTING GREATWOOD GOLD CUP

40

Sunday	Huntingdon	Jump	Turf	Afternoon
05 March 2017	Sedgefield	Jump	Turf	Afternoon

Notes

Monday	Lingfield Park	Jump	Turf	Afternoon
06 March 2017	Southwell	Jump	Turf	Afternoon
	Wolves	Flat	AW	Afternoon

Notes

41

Tuesday	Exeter	Jump	Turf	Afternoon
07 March 2017	Newcastle	Jump	Turf	Afternoon
	Southwell	Flat	AW	Afternoon

Notes

Wednesday	Catterick Bridge	Jump	Turf	Afternoon
08 March 2017	Fontwell Park	Jump	Turf	Afternoon
	Kempton Park	Flat	AW	Twilight
	Lingfield Park	Flat	AW	Afternoon

Notes

42

Thursday	Carlisle	Jump	Turf	Afternoon
09 March 2017	Newcastle	Flat	AW	Evening
	Southwell	Flat	AW	Afternoon
	Wincanton	Jump	Turf	Afternoon

Notes

Friday	Ayr	Jump	Turf	Afternoon
10 March 2017	Leicester	Jump	Turf	Afternoon
	Newcastle	Flat	AW	Evening
	Sandown Park	Jump	Turf	Afternoon

Notes

Saturday

11 March
2017

Ayr	Jump	Turf	Afternoon
Chelmsford City	Flat	AW	Evening
Hereford	Jump	Turf	Afternoon
Sandown Park	Jump	Turf	Afternoon
Wolves	Flat	AW	Afternoon

Notes

THE IMPERIAL CUP HANDICAP HURDLE RACE (CLASS 1)
THE EUROPEAN BREEDERS' FUND 'NATIONAL HUNT'
NOVICES'

Sunday	Market Rasen	Jump	Turf	Afternoon
12 March 2017	Warwick	Jump	Turf	Afternoon

Notes

Monday	Chelmsford City	Flat	AW	Twilight
13 March 2017	Chepstow	Jump	Turf	Afternoon
	Plumpton	Jump	Turf	Afternoon
	Stratford-On-Avon	Jump	Turf	Afternoon

Notes

Tuesday	Cheltenham	Jump	Turf	Afternoon
14 March	Sedgefield	Jump	Turf	Afternoon
2017				
	Southwell	Flat	AW	Afternoon
	Wolves	Flat	AW	Twilight

Notes

THE STAN JAMES CHAMPION HURDLE CHALLENGE TROPHY
(CLASS 1)
THE RACING POST ARKLE CHALLENGE TROPHY STEEPLE
CHASE (CLASS 1)
THE SKY BET SUPREME NOVICES' HURDLE RACE (CLASS 1)
THE ULTIMA HANDICAP STEEPLE CHASE
THE OLBG MARES' HURDLE RACE (CLASS 1)

Wednesday	Cheltenham	Jump	Turf	Afternoon
15 March	Huntingdon	Jump	Turf	Afternoon
2017				
	Newcastle	Flat	AW	Twilight
	Southwell	Flat	AW	Afternoon

Notes
THE BETWAY QUEEN MOTHER CHAMPION STEEPLE CHASE
(CLASS 1)
THE RSA STEEPLE CHASE (CLASS 1)
THE NEPTUNE INVESTMENT MANAGEMENT NOVICES'
HURDLE RACE (CLASS 1)
THE CORAL CUP (A HANDICAP HURDLE RACE) (CLASS 1)
THE WEATHERBYS CHAMPION BUMPER
THE FRED WINTER JUVENILE HANDICAP HURDLE RACE
(CLASS 1)

46

Thursday 16 March 2017	Chelmsford City	Flat	AW	Evening
	Cheltenham	Jump	Turf	Afternoon
	Hexham	Jump	Turf	Afternoon
	Towcester	Jump	Turf	Afternoon

Notes

THE BYRNE GROUP PLATE (A HANDICAP STEEPLE CHASE) (CLASS 1)
THE RYANAIR WORLD HURDLE RACE (CLASS 1)
THE RYANAIR STEEPLE CHASE (CLASS 1)
THE DAWN RUN MARES' NOVICES' HURDLE (CLASS 1)
THE JLT NOVICES' STEEPLE CHASE (CLASS 1)

Friday 17 March 2017 St Patrick's Day	Cheltenham	Jump	Turf	Afternoon
	Fakenham	Jump	Turf	Afternoon
	Lingfield Park	Flat	AW	Afternoon
	Wolves	Flat	AW	Evening

Notes

THE TIMICO CHELTENHAM GOLD CUP STEEPLE CHASE (CLASS 1)
THE JCB TRIUMPH HURDLE RACE (CLASS 1)
THE JOHNNY HENDERSON GRAND ANNUAL STEEPLE CHASE CHALLENGE CUP
THE VINCENT O'BRIEN COUNTY HANDICAP HURDLE RACE (CLASS 1)
THE ALBERT BARTLETT NOVICES' HURDLE RACE (CLASS 1)

47

Saturday

18 March
2017

Fontwell Park	Jump	Turf	Afternoon
Kempton Park	Jump	Turf	Afternoon
Newcastle	Jump	Turf	Afternoon
Uttoxeter	Jump	Turf	Afternoon
Wolves	Flat	AW	Evening

Notes

48

Sunday	Carlisle	Jump	Turf	Afternoon
19 March 2017	Ffos Las	Jump	Turf	Afternoon

Notes

Monday	Kempton Park	Flat	AW	Afternoon
20 March 2017	Southwell	Jump	Turf	Afternoon
	Taunton	Jump	Turf	Afternoon

Notes

Tuesday	Exeter	Jump	Turf	Afternoon
21 March	Southwell	Flat	AW	Afternoon
2017				
	Wetherby	Jump	Turf	Afternoon

Notes

Wednesday	Haydock Park	Jump	Turf	Afternoon
22 March	Kempton Park	Flat	AW	Twilight
2017				
	Newcastle	Flat	AW	Afternoon
	Warwick	Jump	Turf	Afternoon

Notes

50

Thursday	Chelmsford City	Flat	AW	Evening
23 March	Chepstow	Jump	Turf	Afternoon
2017	Ludlow	Jump	Turf	Afternoon
	Wolves	Flat	AW	Afternoon

Notes

Friday	Lingfield Park	Flat	AW	Afternoon
24 March	Musselburgh	Jump	Turf	Afternoon
2017	Newbury	Jump	Turf	Afternoon
	Newcastle	Flat	AW	Evening

Notes

Saturday
25 March
2017

Bangor-On-Dee	Jump	Turf	Afternoon
Kelso	Jump	Turf	Afternoon
Lingfield Park	Flat	AW	Afternoon
Newbury	Jump	Turf	Afternoon
Stratford-On-Avon	Jump	Turf	Afternoon
Wolves	Flat	AW	Evening

Notes

Sunday	Hereford	Jump	Turf	Afternoon
26 March 2017	Wincanton	Jump	Turf	Afternoon

Notes

Monday	Market Rasen	Jump	Turf	Afternoon
27 March 2017	Plumpton	Jump	Turf	Afternoon
	Wolves	Flat	AW	Afternoon

Notes

Tuesday	Hexham	Jump	Turf	Afternoon
28 March 2017	Southwell	Jump	Turf	Afternoon
	Wolves	Flat	AW	Afternoon

Notes

Wednesday	Kempton Park	Flat	AW	Twilight
29 March 2017	Lingfield Park	Flat	AW	Afternoon
	Sedgefield	Jump	Turf	Afternoon
	Southwell	Flat	AW	Afternoon

Notes

Thursday

30 March 2017

Chelmsford City	Flat	AW	Evening
Taunton	Jump	Turf	Afternoon
Warwick	Jump	Turf	Afternoon
Wolves	Flat	AW	Afternoon

Notes

Friday

31 March 2017

Fontwell Park	Jump	Turf	Afternoon
Lingfield Park	Flat	AW	Afternoon
Newcastle	Flat	AW	Evening
Wetherby	Jump	Turf	Afternoon

Notes

Saturday

01 April 2017

Chelmsford City	Flat	AW	Evening
Doncaster	Flat	Turf	Afternoon
Kempton Park	Flat	AW	Afternoon
Stratford-On-Avon	Jump	Turf	Afternoon
Uttoxeter	Jump	Turf	Afternoon

Notes

THE BETWAY LINCOLN (HERITAGE HANDICAP) (CLASS 2)

Sunday 02 April 2017	Ascot	Jump	Turf	Afternoon
	Doncaster	Flat	Turf	Afternoon

Notes

Monday 03 April 2017	Huntingdon	Jump	Turf	Afternoon
	Kelso	Jump	Turf	Afternoon
	Ludlow	Jump	Turf	Afternoon

Notes

Tuesday	Kempton Park	Jump	Turf	Afternoon
04 April 2017	Newton Abbot	Jump	Turf	Afternoon
	Southwell	Flat	AW	Afternoon

Notes

Wednesday	Carlisle	Jump	Turf	Afternoon
05 April 2017	Kempton Park	Flat	AW	Twilight
	Wincanton	Jump	Turf	Afternoon
	Wolves	Flat	AW	Afternoon

Notes

Thursday 06 April 2017	Aintree	Jump	Turf	Afternoon
	Chelmsford City	Flat	AW	Evening
	Southwell	Flat	AW	Afternoon
	Taunton	Jump	Turf	Afternoon

Notes
THE BETFRED ANNIVERSARY 4-Y-O JUVENILE HURDLE RACE (CLASS 1)
THE BETFRED BOWL STEEPLE CHASE (CLASS 1)
THE DOOM BAR AINTREE HURDLE (CLASS 1)
THE BETFRED RED RUM HANDICAP STEEPLE CHASE (CLASS 1)
THE MERSEYRAIL MANIFESTO NOVICES' STEEPLE CHASE
THE NICKEL COIN MARES' STANDARD OPEN

Friday 07 April 2017	Aintree	Jump	Turf	Afternoon
	Kempton Park	Flat	AW	Evening
	Leicester	Flat	Turf	Afternoon
	Sedgefield	Jump	Turf	Afternoon

Notes
THE CRABBIE'S TOPHAM STEEPLE CHASE (HANDICAP) (CLASS 1)
THE TOP NOVICES' HURDLE RACE (CLASS 1)
THE JLT MELLING STEEPLE CHASE (CLASS 1)
THE BETFRED MILDMAY NOVICES' STEEPLE CHASE (CLASS 1)
THE ALDER HEY CHILDREN'S CHARITY HANDICAP HURDLE RACE (CLASS 1)
THE DOOM BAR SEFTON NOVICES' HURDLE RACE (CLASS 1)
THE WEATHERBYS PRIVATE BANKING CHAMPION STANDARD OPEN

Saturday	Aintree	Jump	Turf	Afternoon
08 April 2017	Chepstow	Jump	Turf	Afternoon
	Lingfield Park	Flat	AW	Afternoon
	Newcastle	Jump	Turf	Afternoon
	Wolves	Flat	AW	Evening

Notes

THE GASKELLS WASTE MANAGEMENT HANDICAP HURDLE RACE (CLASS 1)

THE LIVERPOOL STAYERS' HURDLE RACE (CLASS 1)

THE DOOM BAR MAGHULL NOVICES' STEEPLE CHASE (CLASS 1)

THE CRABBIE'S GRAND NATIONAL STEEPLE CHASE (HANDICAP)

THE MERSEY NOVICES' HURDLE RACE (CLASS 1)

Sunday	Ffos Las	Jump	Turf	Afternoon
09 April 2017	Market Rasen	Jump	Turf	Afternoon

Notes

Monday	Kelso	Jump	Turf	Afternoon
10 April 2017	Redcar	Flat	Turf	Afternoon
	Windsor	Flat	Turf	Afternoon

Notes

Tuesday	Exeter	Jump	Turf	Afternoon
11 April	Lingfield Park	Flat	AW	Afternoon
2017				
	Pontefract	Flat	Turf	Afternoon

Notes

Wednesday	Catterick Bridge	Flat	Turf	Afternoon
12 April	Fontwell Park	Jump	Turf	Afternoon
2017				
	Kempton Park	Flat	AW	Twilight
	Nottingham	Flat	Turf	Afternoon

Notes

Thursday	Chelmsford City	Flat	AW	Afternoon
13 April 2017	Towcester	Jump	Turf	Afternoon
	Wetherby	Jump	Turf	Afternoon

Notes

Friday	Bath	Flat	Turf	Afternoon
14 April 2017	Lingfield Park	Flat	AW	Afternoon
	Newcastle	Flat	AW	Afternoon

Good Friday

Notes

Saturday

15 April 2017

Brighton	Flat	Turf	Evening
Carlisle	Jump	Turf	Afternoon
Haydock Park	Jump	Turf	Afternoon
Kempton Park	Flat	AW	Afternoon
Musselburgh	Flat	Turf	Afternoon
Newton Abbot	Jump	Turf	Afternoon
Stratford-On-Avon	Jump	Turf	Evening

Notes

Sunday	Ffos Las	Jump	Turf	Afternoon
16 April 2017	Plumpton	Jump	Turf	Afternoon
	Southwell	Flat	AW	Afternoon

Notes

Monday	Chepstow	Jump	Turf	Afternoon
17 April 2017	Fakenham	Jump	Turf	Afternoon
	Huntingdon	Jump	Turf	Afternoon
	Market Rasen	Jump	Turf	Afternoon
	Plumpton	Jump	Turf	Afternoon
	Redcar	Flat	Turf	Afternoon
	Wolves	Flat	AW	Afternoon

Easter Monday

Notes

Tuesday	Exeter	Jump	Turf	Evening
18 April 2017	Kempton Park	Jump	Turf	Afternoon
	Ludlow	Jump	Turf	Evening
	Newmarket	Flat	Turf	Afternoon
	Southwell	Flat	AW	Afternoon

Notes

Wednesday	Beverley	Flat	Turf	Afternoon
19 April 2017	Cheltenham	Jump	Turf	Afternoon
	Newmarket	Flat	Turf	Afternoon
	Sedgefield	Jump	Turf	Evening
	Wolves	Flat	AW	Evening

Notes

Thursday	Cheltenham	Jump	Turf	Afternoon
20 April 2017	Lingfield Park	Flat	AW	Evening
	Newmarket	Flat	Turf	Afternoon
	Ripon	Flat	Turf	Afternoon
	Taunton	Jump	Turf	Evening

Notes

Friday	Ayr	Jump	Turf	Afternoon
21 April 2017	Bath	Flat	Turf	Evening
	Fontwell Park	Jump	Turf	Afternoon
	Newbury	Flat	Turf	Afternoon
	Southwell	Jump	Turf	Evening

Notes

Saturday

22 April
2017

Ayr	Jump	Turf	Afternoon
Bangor-On-Dee	Jump	Turf	Afternoon
Newbury	Flat	Turf	Afternoon
Nottingham	Flat	Turf	Evening
Thirsk	Flat	Turf	Afternoon
Wolves	Flat	AW	Evening

Notes

Sunday	Stratford-On-Avon	Jump	Turf	Afternoon
23 April	Wetherby	Jump	Turf	Afternoon
2017	Wincanton	Jump	Turf	Afternoon

Notes

Monday	Kempton Park	Flat	AW	Afternoon
24 April	Lingfield Park	Flat	AW	Evening
2017	Pontefract	Flat	Turf	Afternoon
	Warwick	Jump	Turf	Afternoon
	Windsor	Flat	Turf	Evening

Notes

69

Tuesday	Brighton	Flat	Turf	Evening
25 April 2017	Hexham	Jump	Turf	Afternoon
	Ludlow	Jump	Turf	Afternoon
	Wolves	Flat	AW	Evening
	Yarmouth	Flat	Turf	Afternoon

Notes

Wednesday	Catterick Bridge	Flat	Turf	Afternoon
26 April 2017	Epsom Downs	Flat	Turf	Afternoon
	Exeter	Jump	Turf	Evening
	Lingfield Park	Flat	AW	Evening
	Perth	Jump	Turf	Afternoon

Notes

Thursday 27 April 2017	Beverley	Flat	Turf	Afternoon
	Chelmsford City	Flat	AW	Evening
	Market Rasen	Jump	Turf	Evening
	Perth	Jump	Turf	Afternoon
	Taunton	Jump	Turf	Afternoon

Notes

Friday 28 April 2017	Chepstow	Jump	Turf	Evening
	Doncaster	Flat	Turf	Afternoon
	Huntingdon	Jump	Turf	Evening
	Perth	Jump	Turf	Afternoon
	Sandown Park	Flat	Turf	Afternoon

Notes

Saturday

29 April
2017

Doncaster	Flat	Turf	Evening
Haydock Park	Flat	Turf	Afternoon
Leicester	Flat	Turf	Afternoon
Ripon	Flat	Turf	Afternoon
Sandown Park	Jump	Turf	Afternoon
Wolves	Flat	AW	Evening

Notes

THE bet365 CELEBRATION STEEPLE CHASE (CLASS 1)

Sunday	Salisbury	Flat	Turf	Afternoon
30 April	Thirsk	Flat	Turf	Afternoon
2017				

Notes

Monday	Bath	Flat	Turf	Afternoon
01 May	Beverley	Flat	Turf	Afternoon
2017				
	Kempton Park	Jump	Turf	Afternoon
	Warwick	Jump	Turf	Afternoon
Early May Bank Holiday	Windsor	Flat	Turf	Afternoon

Notes

Tuesday	Brighton	Flat	Turf	Afternoon
02 May	Chelmsford City	Flat	AW	Evening
2017	Nottingham	Flat	Turf	Afternoon
	Wolves	Flat	AW	Evening
	Yarmouth	Flat	Turf	Afternoon

Notes

Wednesday	Ascot	Flat	Turf	Afternoon
03 May	Brighton	Flat	Turf	Evening
2017	Pontefract	Flat	Turf	Afternoon
	Wolves	Flat	AW	Afternoon
	Yarmouth	Flat	Turf	Evening

Notes

Thursday	Lingfield Park	Flat	AW	Afternoon
04 May 2017	Musselburgh	Flat	Turf	Evening
	Redcar	Flat	Turf	Afternoon
	Sedgefield	Jump	Turf	Evening
	Towcester	Jump	Turf	Afternoon

Notes

Friday	Cheltenham	Jump	Turf	Evening
05 May 2017	Chepstow	Flat	Turf	Afternoon
	Fontwell Park	Jump	Turf	Evening
	Lingfield Park	Flat	AW	Afternoon
	Musselburgh	Flat	Turf	Afternoon

Notes

Saturday	Doncaster	Flat	Turf	Evening
06 May 2017	Goodwood	Flat	Turf	Afternoon
	Hexham	Jump	Turf	Evening
	Newmarket	Flat	Turf	Afternoon
	Thirsk	Flat	Turf	Afternoon
	Uttoxeter	Jump	Turf	Afternoon

Notes

THE JOCKEY CLUB STAKES (CLASS 1)

THE QIPCO 2000 GUINEAS STAKES (CLASS 1)

THE PEARL BLOODSTOCK PALACE HOUSE STAKES (CLASS 1)

Sunday	Hamilton Park	Flat	Turf	Afternoon
07 May 2017	Newmarket	Flat	Turf	Afternoon

Notes

THE QIPCO 1000 GUINEAS STAKES (CLASS 1)

THE QATAR BLOODSTOCK DAHLIA STAKES (CLASS 1)

Monday	Ayr	Flat	Turf	Afternoon
08 May 2017	Chelmsford City	Flat	AW	Evening
	Southwell	Flat	AW	Afternoon
	Stratford-On-Avon	Jump	Turf	Afternoon
	Windsor	Flat	Turf	Evening

Notes

Tuesday	Ayr	Flat	Turf	Afternoon
09 May	Exeter	Jump	Turf	Evening
2017				
	Fakenham	Jump	Turf	Afternoon
	Ffos Las	Jump	Turf	Afternoon
	Leicester	Flat	Turf	Evening

Notes

Wednesday	Bath	Flat	Turf	Evening
10 May	Chelmsford City	Flat	AW	Evening
2017				
	Chester	Flat	Turf	Afternoon
	Kelso	Jump	Turf	Afternoon
	Newton Abbot	Jump	Turf	Afternoon

Notes

THE BETWAY CHESTER CUP (CLASS 2 HERITAGE HANDICAP)

Thursday	Carlisle	Jump	Turf	Evening
11 May	Catterick Bridge	Flat	Turf	Afternoon
2017	Chester	Flat	Turf	Afternoon
	Wincanton	Jump	Turf	Evening
	Worcester	Jump	Turf	Afternoon

Notes

Friday	Ascot	Flat	Turf	Evening
12 May	Chester	Flat	Turf	Afternoon
2017	Lingfield Park	Flat	Turf	Afternoon
	Market Rasen	Jump	Turf	Afternoon
	Nottingham	Flat	Turf	Evening
	Ripon	Flat	Turf	Evening

Notes

Saturday

13 May

2017

Ascot	Flat	Turf	Afternoon
Haydock Park	Mixed	Turf	Afternoon
Hexham	Jump	Turf	Afternoon
Lingfield Park	Flat	Turf	Afternoon
Nottingham	Flat	Turf	Afternoon
Thirsk	Flat	Turf	Evening
Warwick	Jump	Turf	Evening

Notes

THE Totescoop6 VICTORIA CUP

THE SWINTON HANDICAP HURDLE RACE (CLASS 1)

THE CHARTWELL FILLIES' STAKES (CLASS 1)

Sunday	Ludlow	Jump	Turf	Afternoon
14 May 2017	Plumpton	Jump	Turf	Afternoon

Notes

Monday	Brighton	Flat	Turf	Afternoon
15 May 2017	Kempton Park	Jump	Turf	Afternoon
	Towcester	Jump	Turf	Evening
	Wetherby	Flat	Turf	Afternoon
	Windsor	Flat	Turf	Evening

Notes

Tuesday	Beverley	Flat	Turf	Afternoon
16 May 2017	Chepstow	Flat	Turf	Evening
	Sedgefield	Jump	Turf	Afternoon
	Southwell	Jump	Turf	Evening
	Wincanton	Jump	Turf	Afternoon

Notes

Wednesday	Bath	Flat	Turf	Evening
17 May 2017	Perth	Jump	Turf	Evening
	Worcester	Jump	Turf	Afternoon
	Yarmouth	Flat	Turf	Afternoon
	York	Flat	Turf	Afternoon

Notes

Thursday	Fontwell Park	Jump	Turf	Evening
18 May 2017	Newmarket	Flat	Turf	Evening
	Perth	Jump	Turf	Afternoon
	Salisbury	Flat	Turf	Afternoon
	York	Flat	Turf	Afternoon

Notes

Friday	Aintree	Jump	Turf	Evening
19 May 2017	Hamilton Park	Flat	Turf	Evening
	Newbury	Flat	Turf	Afternoon
	Newcastle	Flat	AW	Evening
	Newmarket	Flat	Turf	Afternoon
	York	Flat	Turf	Afternoon

Notes

THE BETWAY YORKSHIRE CUP (CLASS 1)

Saturday

20 May 2017

Bangor-On-Dee	Jump	Turf	Afternoon
Doncaster	Flat	Turf	Evening
Newbury	Flat	Turf	Afternoon
Newmarket	Flat	Turf	Afternoon
Thirsk	Flat	Turf	Afternoon
Uttoxeter	Jump	Turf	Evening

Notes

Sunday	Market Rasen	Jump	Turf	Afternoon
21 May 2017	Ripon	Flat	Turf	Afternoon
	Stratford-On-Avon	Jump	Turf	Afternoon

Notes

Monday	Carlisle	Flat	Turf	Afternoon
22 May 2017	Leicester	Flat	Turf	Evening
	Redcar	Flat	Turf	Afternoon
	Towcester	Jump	Turf	Afternoon
	Windsor	Flat	Turf	Evening

Notes

Tuesday	Brighton	Flat	Turf	Afternoon
23 May 2017	Hexham	Jump	Turf	Evening
	Huntingdon	Jump	Turf	Evening
	Newcastle	Flat	AW	Afternoon
	Nottingham	Flat	Turf	Afternoon

Notes

Wednesday	Ayr	Flat	Turf	Afternoon
24 May 2017	Kempton Park	Flat	AW	Evening
	Lingfield Park	Flat	Turf	Afternoon
	Southwell	Jump	Turf	Evening
	Yarmouth	Flat	Turf	Afternoon

Notes

Thursday 25 May 2017	Catterick Bridge	Flat	Turf	Afternoon
	Chelmsford City	Flat	AW	Evening
	Goodwood	Flat	Turf	Afternoon
	Sandown Park	Flat	Turf	Evening
	Warwick	Jump	Turf	Afternoon

Notes

Friday 26 May 2017	Bath	Flat	Turf	Afternoon
	Goodwood	Flat	Turf	Afternoon
	Haydock Park	Flat	Turf	Afternoon
	Musselburgh	Flat	Turf	Evening
	Pontefract	Flat	Turf	Evening
	Worcester	Jump	Turf	Evening

Notes

Saturday

27 May 2017

Cartmel	Jump	Turf	Afternoon
Chester	Flat	Turf	Afternoon
Ffos Las	Jump	Turf	Evening
Goodwood	Flat	Turf	Afternoon
Haydock Park	Flat	Turf	Afternoon
Salisbury	Flat	Turf	Evening
York	Flat	Turf	Afternoon

Notes

88

Sunday	Fontwell Park	Jump	Turf	Afternoon
28 May 2017	Kelso	Jump	Turf	Afternoon
	Uttoxeter	Jump	Turf	Afternoon

Notes

Monday	Cartmel	Jump	Turf	Afternoon
29 May 2017	Chelmsford City	Flat	AW	Afternoon
	Huntingdon	Jump	Turf	Afternoon
	Leicester	Flat	Turf	Afternoon
Spring Bank Holiday	Redcar	Flat	Turf	Afternoon
	Windsor	Flat	Turf	Afternoon

Notes

Tuesday 30 May 2017	Leicester	Flat	Turf	Afternoon
	Lingfield Park	Flat	AW	Afternoon
	Newton Abbot	Jump	Turf	Evening
	Redcar	Flat	Turf	Afternoon
	Wolves	Flat	AW	Evening

Notes

Wednesday 31 May 2017	Ayr	Flat	Turf	Evening
	Beverley	Flat	Turf	Afternoon
	Cartmel	Jump	Turf	Afternoon
	Kempton Park	Flat	AW	Evening
	Nottingham	Flat	Turf	Afternoon

Notes

Thursday 01 June 2017	Chelmsford City	Flat	AW	Evening
	Ffos Las	Jump	Turf	Evening
	Hamilton Park	Flat	Turf	Afternoon
	Lingfield Park	Flat	Turf	Afternoon
	Newcastle	Flat	AW	Evening
	Wolves	Flat	AW	Afternoon

Notes

Friday 02 June 2017	Bath	Flat	Turf	Evening
	Catterick Bridge	Flat	Turf	Afternoon
	Doncaster	Flat	Turf	Evening
	Epsom Downs	Flat	Turf	Afternoon
	Goodwood	Flat	Turf	Evening
	Market Rasen	Jump	Turf	Afternoon

Notes

THE INVESTEC OAKS (CLASS 1)

Saturday

03 June 2017

Doncaster	Flat	Turf	Afternoon
Epsom Downs	Flat	Turf	Afternoon
Hexham	Jump	Turf	Afternoon
Lingfield Park	Flat	Turf	Evening
Musselburgh	Flat	Turf	Afternoon
Newcastle	Flat	AW	Evening
Worcester	Jump	Turf	Afternoon

Notes

THE PRINCESS ELIZABETH STAKES (CLASS 1)

THE INVESTEC CORONATION CUP (CLASS 1)

THE INVESTEC DERBY (CLASS 1)

THE INVESTEC CORPORATE BANKING 'DASH' (HERITAGE HANDICAP) (CLASS 2)

Sunday	Fakenham	Jump	Turf	Afternoon
04 June 2017	Perth	Jump	Turf	Afternoon

Notes

Monday	Ayr	Flat	Turf	Evening
05 June 2017	Leicester	Flat	Turf	Afternoon
	Newton Abbot	Jump	Turf	Afternoon
	Thirsk	Flat	Turf	Afternoon
	Windsor	Flat	Turf	Evening

Notes

Tuesday	Chepstow	Flat	Turf	Afternoon
06 June 2017	Fontwell Park	Jump	Turf	Evening
	Southwell	Jump	Turf	Evening
	Wetherby	Flat	Turf	Afternoon
	Yarmouth	Flat	Turf	Afternoon

Notes

Wednesday	Hamilton Park	Flat	Turf	Afternoon
07 June 2017	Kempton Park	Flat	AW	Evening
	Ripon	Flat	Turf	Evening
	Uttoxeter	Jump	Turf	Afternoon
	Wolves	Flat	AW	Afternoon

Notes

94

Thursday	Bangor-On-Dee	Jump	Turf	Afternoon
08 June 2017	Carlisle	Flat	Turf	Evening
	Haydock Park	Flat	Turf	Afternoon
	Ripon	Flat	Turf	Afternoon
	Sandown Park	Flat	Turf	Evening

Notes

Friday	Brighton	Flat	Turf	Afternoon
09 June 2017	Carlisle	Flat	Turf	Afternoon
	Goodwood	Flat	Turf	Evening
	Haydock Park	Flat	Turf	Evening
	Stratford-On-Avon	Jump	Turf	Evening
	Wolves	Flat	AW	Afternoon

Notes

Saturday

10 June 2017

Beverley	Flat	Turf	Afternoon
Catterick Bridge	Flat	Turf	Afternoon
Chepstow	Flat	Turf	Evening
Chester	Flat	Turf	Afternoon
Haydock Park	Flat	Turf	Afternoon
Newmarket	Flat	Turf	Afternoon
Stratford-On-Avon	Jump	Turf	Evening

Notes

Sunday	Goodwood	Flat	Turf	Afternoon
11 June 2017	Nottingham	Flat	Turf	Afternoon

Notes

Monday	Ayr	Flat	Turf	Afternoon
12 June 2017	Brighton	Flat	Turf	Afternoon
	Pontefract	Flat	Turf	Evening
	Windsor	Flat	Turf	Evening

Notes

Tuesday	Lingfield Park	Flat	Turf	Evening
13 June 2017	Salisbury	Flat	Turf	Afternoon
	Southwell	Jump	Turf	Evening
	Yarmouth	Flat	Turf	Afternoon

Notes

Wednesday	Hamilton Park	Flat	Turf	Evening
14 June 2017	Haydock Park	Flat	Turf	Afternoon
	Kempton Park	Flat	AW	Evening
	Worcester	Jump	Turf	Afternoon
	Yarmouth	Flat	Turf	Afternoon

Notes

Thursday	Fontwell Park	Jump	Turf	Afternoon
15 June	Haydock Park	Flat	Turf	Evening
2017	Newbury	Flat	Turf	Afternoon
	Nottingham	Flat	Turf	Afternoon
	Uttoxeter	Jump	Turf	Evening

Notes

Friday	Aintree	Jump	Turf	Evening
16 June	Chepstow	Flat	Turf	Evening
2017	Goodwood	Flat	Turf	Evening
	Newton Abbot	Jump	Turf	Afternoon
	Sandown Park	Flat	Turf	Afternoon
	York	Flat	Turf	Afternoon

Notes

Saturday	Bath	Flat	Turf	Afternoon
17 June 2017	Hexham	Jump	Turf	Afternoon
	Leicester	Flat	Turf	Evening
	Lingfield Park	Flat	Turf	Evening
	Musselburgh	Flat	Turf	Afternoon
	Sandown Park	Flat	Turf	Afternoon
	York	Flat	Turf	Afternoon

Notes

THE WILLIAM HILL SCOTTISH SPRINT CUP (A HERITAGE HANDICAP)

100

Sunday	Doncaster	Flat	Turf	Afternoon
18 June 2017	Salisbury	Flat	Turf	Afternoon

Notes

Monday	Carlisle	Flat	Turf	Afternoon
19 June 2017	Nottingham	Flat	Turf	Evening
	Wetherby	Flat	Turf	Afternoon
	Windsor	Flat	Turf	Evening

Notes

Tuesday	Ascot	Flat	Turf	Afternoon
20 June 2017	Beverley	Flat	Turf	Evening
	Brighton	Flat	Turf	Evening
	Stratford-On-Avon	Jump	Turf	Afternoon
	Thirsk	Flat	Turf	Afternoon

Notes

THE ST JAMES'S PALACE STAKES (CLASS 1)

THE QUEEN ANNE STAKES (CLASS 1)

THE COVENTRY STAKES (CLASS 1)

THE KING'S STAND STAKES (CLASS 1)

Wednesday	Ascot	Flat	Turf	Afternoon
21 June 2017	Chelmsford City	Flat	AW	Evening
	Hamilton Park	Flat	Turf	Afternoon
	Ripon	Flat	Turf	Evening
	Uttoxeter	Jump	Turf	Afternoon

THE PRINCE OF WALES'S STAKES (CLASS 1)
THE JERSEY STAKES (CLASS 1)
THE QUEEN MARY STAKES (CLASS 1)
THE DUKE OF CAMBRIDGE STAKES (CLASS 1)
THE ROYAL HUNT CUP (CLASS 2 HERITAGE HANDICAP)

Thursday	Ascot	Flat	Turf	Afternoon
22 June 2017	Chelmsford City	Flat	AW	Afternoon
	Ffos Las	Jump	Turf	Evening
	Lingfield Park	Flat	AW	Evening
	Ripon	Flat	Turf	Afternoon

Notes

THE GOLD CUP (CLASS 1)

THE RIBBLESDALE STAKES (CLASS 1)

THE NORFOLK STAKES (CLASS 1)

THE TERCENTENARY STAKES (CLASS 1)

THE BRITANNIA STAKES (CLASS 2 HERITAGE HANDICAP)

Friday	Ascot	Flat	Turf	Afternoon
23 June 2017	Ayr	Flat	Turf	Evening
	Bath	Flat	Turf	Evening
	Market Rasen	Jump	Turf	Afternoon
	Newmarket	Flat	Turf	Evening
	Redcar	Flat	Turf	Afternoon

Notes

THE KING EDWARD VII STAKES (CLASS 1)

THE CORONATION STAKES (CLASS 1)

THE ALBANY STAKES (CLASS 1)

THE COMMONWEALTH CUP (CLASS 1)

Saturday	Ascot	Flat	Turf	Afternoon
24 June 2017	Ayr	Flat	Turf	Afternoon
	Haydock Park	Flat	Turf	Evening
	Lingfield Park	Flat	Turf	Evening
	Newmarket	Flat	Turf	Afternoon
	Redcar	Flat	Turf	Afternoon

Notes

THE DIAMOND JUBILEE STAKES (CLASS 1)

THE HARDWICKE STAKES (CLASS 1)

THE WOKINGHAM STAKES (CLASS 2 HERITAGE HANDICAP)

Sunday	Hexham	Jump	Turf	Afternoon
25 June 2017	Pontefract	Flat	Turf	Afternoon
	Worcester	Jump	Turf	Afternoon

Notes

Monday	Chepstow	Flat	Turf	Afternoon
26 June 2017	Southwell	Jump	Turf	Evening
	Windsor	Flat	Turf	Evening
	Wolves	Flat	AW	Afternoon

Notes

Tuesday
27 June
2017

Beverley	Flat	Turf	Afternoon
Brighton	Flat	Turf	Afternoon
Leicester	Flat	Turf	Evening
Newton Abbot	Jump	Turf	Evening

Notes

Wednesday
28 June
2017

Bath	Flat	Turf	Evening
Carlisle	Flat	Turf	Afternoon
Kempton Park	Flat	AW	Evening
Salisbury	Flat	Turf	Afternoon
Worcester	Jump	Turf	Afternoon

Notes

Thursday **29 June** **2017**	Hamilton Park	Flat	Turf	Evening
	Newbury	Flat	Turf	Evening
	Newcastle	Flat	AW	Afternoon
	Newmarket	Flat	Turf	Afternoon
	Nottingham	Flat	Turf	Afternoon

Notes

Friday **30 June** **2017**	Cartmel	Jump	Turf	Afternoon
	Chester	Flat	Turf	Evening
	Doncaster	Flat	Turf	Afternoon
	Newcastle	Flat	AW	Evening
	Newmarket	Flat	Turf	Evening
	Yarmouth	Flat	Turf	Afternoon

Notes

Saturday	Chester	Flat	Turf	Afternoon
01 July	Doncaster	Flat	Turf	Evening
2017				
	Lingfield Park	Flat	Turf	Evening
	Newcastle	Flat	AW	Afternoon
	Newmarket	Flat	Turf	Afternoon
	Windsor	Flat	Turf	Afternoon
	York	Flat	Turf	Afternoon

Notes

Sunday

02 July 2017

Cartmel	Jump	Turf	Afternoon
Uttoxeter	Jump	Turf	Afternoon
Windsor	Flat	Turf	Afternoon

Notes

Monday

03 July 2017

Hamilton Park	Flat	Turf	Evening
Pontefract	Flat	Turf	Afternoon
Windsor	Flat	Turf	Evening
Wolves	Flat	AW	Afternoon

Notes

Tuesday	Brighton	Flat	Turf	Afternoon
04 July 2017	Chepstow	Flat	Turf	Evening
	Hamilton Park	Flat	Turf	Afternoon
	Stratford-On-Avon	Jump	Turf	Evening

Notes

Wednesday	Bath	Flat	Turf	Evening
05 July 2017	Kempton Park	Flat	AW	Evening
	Perth	Jump	Turf	Afternoon
	Thirsk	Flat	Turf	Afternoon
	Worcester	Jump	Turf	Afternoon

Notes

Thursday	Epsom Downs	Flat	Turf	Evening
06 July 2017	Haydock Park	Flat	Turf	Afternoon
	Newbury	Flat	Turf	Evening
	Perth	Jump	Turf	Afternoon
	Yarmouth	Flat	Turf	Afternoon

Notes

Friday	Beverley	Flat	Turf	Evening
07 July 2017	Chelmsford City	Flat	AW	Evening
	Doncaster	Flat	Turf	Afternoon
	Haydock Park	Flat	Turf	Evening
	Newton Abbot	Jump	Turf	Afternoon
	Sandown Park	Flat	Turf	Afternoon

Notes

Saturday

08 July 2017

Beverley	Flat	Turf	Afternoon
Carlisle	Flat	Turf	Evening
Haydock Park	Flat	Turf	Afternoon
Leicester	Flat	Turf	Afternoon
Nottingham	Flat	Turf	Evening
Sandown Park	Flat	Turf	Afternoon

Notes

THE bet365 LANCASHIRE OAKS (CLASS 1)

THE bet365 OLD NEWTON CUP (CLASS 2 HERITAGE HANDICAP)
THE CORAL-ECLIPSE (CLASS 1) (BRITISH CHAMPIONS SERIES)
THE CORAL CHARGE (CLASS 1)

Sunday

09 July
2017

| Ayr | Flat | Turf | Afternoon |
| Market Rasen | Jump | Turf | Afternoon |

Notes

Monday

10 July
2017

Ayr	Flat	Turf	Afternoon
Ripon	Flat	Turf	Evening
Windsor	Flat	Turf	Evening
Worcester	Jump	Turf	Afternoon

Notes

Tuesday	Brighton	Flat	Turf	Evening
11 July	Pontefract	Flat	Turf	Afternoon
2017	Uttoxeter	Jump	Turf	Evening
	Wolves	Flat	AW	Afternoon

Notes

Wednesday	Bath	Flat	Turf	Evening
12 July	Catterick Bridge	Flat	Turf	Afternoon
2017	Kempton Park	Flat	AW	Evening
	Lingfield Park	Flat	Turf	Afternoon
	Yarmouth	Flat	Turf	Afternoon

Notes

114

Thursday 13 July 2017				
	Carlisle	Flat	Turf	Afternoon
	Doncaster	Flat	Turf	Afternoon
	Epsom Downs	Flat	Turf	Evening
	Newbury	Flat	Turf	Evening
	Newmarket	Flat	Turf	Afternoon

Notes

Friday 14 July 2017				
	Ascot	Flat	Turf	Afternoon
	Carlisle	Flat	Turf	Evening
	Chepstow	Flat	Turf	Evening
	Musselburgh	Flat	Turf	Evening
	Newmarket	Flat	Turf	Afternoon
	York	Flat	Turf	Afternoon

Notes

THE DUCHESS OF CAMBRIDGE STAKES (CLASS 1)

THE FALMOUTH STAKES (BRITISH CHAMPIONS SERIES)

THE SUMMER STAKES (CLASS 1)

Saturday	Ascot	Flat	Turf	Afternoon
15 July	Chester	Flat	Turf	Afternoon
2017	Hamilton Park	Flat	Turf	Evening
	Newmarket	Flat	Turf	Afternoon
	Salisbury	Flat	Turf	Evening
	York	Flat	Turf	Afternoon

Notes

THE 56th JOHN SMITH'S CUP (CLASS 2 HERITAGE HANDICAP)

THE FRED COWLEY MBE MEMORIAL SUMMER MILE STAKES (CLASS 1)

THE Totepool HERITAGE HANDICAP STAKES (CLASS 2)

THE DARLEY JULY CUP (CLASS 1)

THE Bet365 SUPERLATIVE STAKES (CLASS 1)

THE Bet365 BUNBURY CUP (CLASS 2 HERITAGE HANDICAP)

Sunday	Perth	Jump	Turf	Afternoon
16 July 2017	Southwell	Jump	Turf	Afternoon
	Stratford-On-Avon	Jump	Turf	Afternoon

Notes

Monday	Ayr	Flat	Turf	Afternoon
17 July 2017	Ffos Las	Flat	Turf	Afternoon
	Windsor	Flat	Turf	Evening
	Wolves	Flat	AW	Evening

Notes

Tuesday 18 July 2017				
	Bath	Flat	Turf	Afternoon
	Beverley	Flat	Turf	Afternoon
	Thirsk	Flat	Turf	Evening
	Worcester	Jump	Turf	Evening

Notes

Wednesday 19 July 2017				
	Catterick Bridge	Flat	Turf	Afternoon
	Lingfield Park	Flat	Turf	Afternoon
	Sandown Park	Flat	Turf	Evening
	Uttoxeter	Jump	Turf	Afternoon
	Yarmouth	Flat	Turf	Evening

Notes

Thursday	Chepstow	Flat	Turf	Afternoon
20 July	Doncaster	Flat	Turf	Evening
2017				
	Epsom Downs	Flat	Turf	Evening
	Hamilton Park	Flat	Turf	Afternoon
	Leicester	Flat	Turf	Afternoon

Notes

Friday	Hamilton Park	Flat	Turf	Evening
21 July	Haydock Park	Flat	Turf	Afternoon
2017				
	Newbury	Flat	Turf	Afternoon
	Newmarket	Flat	Turf	Evening
	Nottingham	Flat	Turf	Afternoon
	Pontefract	Flat	Turf	Evening

Notes

119

Saturday

22 July 2017

Course	Type	Surface	Time
Cartmel	Jump	Turf	Afternoon
Haydock Park	Flat	Turf	Evening
Lingfield Park	Flat	Turf	Evening
Market Rasen	Jump	Turf	Afternoon
Newbury	Flat	Turf	Afternoon
Newmarket	Flat	Turf	Afternoon
Ripon	Flat	Turf	Afternoon

Notes

120

Sunday	Newton Abbot	Jump	Turf	Afternoon
23 July 2017	Redcar	Flat	Turf	Afternoon
	Stratford-On-Avon	Jump	Turf	Afternoon

Notes

Monday	Ayr	Flat	Turf	Afternoon
24 July 2017	Beverley	Flat	Turf	Evening
	Cartmel	Jump	Turf	Afternoon
	Windsor	Flat	Turf	Evening

Notes

Tuesday	Chelmsford City	Flat	AW	Evening
25 July	Ffos Las	Flat	Turf	Afternoon
2017				
	Musselburgh	Flat	Turf	Afternoon
	Nottingham	Flat	Turf	Evening

Notes

Wednesday	Bath	Flat	Turf	Afternoon
26 July	Catterick Bridge	Flat	Turf	Afternoon
2017	Leicester	Flat	Turf	Evening
	Lingfield Park	Flat	Turf	Afternoon
	Sandown Park	Flat	Turf	Evening

Notes

Thursday	Doncaster	Flat	Turf	Evening
27 July	Newbury	Flat	Turf	Evening
2017	Sandown Park	Flat	Turf	Afternoon
	Worcester	Jump	Turf	Afternoon
	Yarmouth	Flat	Turf	Afternoon

Notes

Friday	Ascot	Flat	Turf	Afternoon
28 July	Chepstow	Flat	Turf	Evening
2017	Newmarket	Flat	Turf	Evening
	Thirsk	Flat	Turf	Afternoon
	Uttoxeter	Jump	Turf	Afternoon
	York	Flat	Turf	Evening

Notes

Saturday	Ascot	Flat	Turf	Afternoon
29 July 2017	Chester	Flat	Turf	Afternoon
	Lingfield Park	Flat	Turf	Evening
	Newcastle	Flat	AW	Afternoon
	Newmarket	Flat	Turf	Afternoon
	Salisbury	Flat	Turf	Evening
	York	Flat	Turf	Afternoon

Notes

THE KING GEORGE VI AND QUEEN ELIZABETH STAKES (CLASS 1)

THE PRINCESS MARGARET JUDDMONTE STAKES (CLASS 1)

THE GIGASET INTERNATIONAL STAKES (CLASS 2 HERITAGE HANDICAP)

THE SKY BET YORK STAKES (CLASS 1)

Sunday	Pontefract	Flat	Turf	Afternoon
30 July 2017	Uttoxeter	Jump	Turf	Afternoon

Notes

Monday	Ayr	Flat	Turf	Afternoon
31 July 2017	Newton Abbot	Jump	Turf	Afternoon
	Windsor	Flat	Turf	Evening
	Wolves	Flat	AW	Evening

Notes

Tuesday	Beverley	Flat	Turf	Afternoon
01 August 2017	Goodwood	Flat	Turf	Afternoon
	Perth	Jump	Turf	Evening
	Worcester	Jump	Turf	Evening
	Yarmouth	Flat	Turf	Afternoon

Notes

Wednesday	Goodwood	Flat	Turf	Afternoon
02 August 2017	Leicester	Flat	Turf	Evening
	Perth	Jump	Turf	Afternoon
	Redcar	Flat	Turf	Afternoon
	Sandown Park	Flat	Turf	Evening

Notes

Thursday	Epsom Downs	Flat	Turf	Evening
03 August 2017	Ffos Las	Flat	Turf	Evening
	Goodwood	Flat	Turf	Afternoon
	Nottingham	Flat	Turf	Afternoon
	Stratford-On-Avon	Jump	Turf	Afternoon

Notes

Friday	Bangor-On-Dee	Jump	Turf	Afternoon
04 August 2017	Bath	Flat	Turf	Evening
	Goodwood	Flat	Turf	Afternoon
	Musselburgh	Flat	Turf	Evening
	Newmarket	Flat	Turf	Evening
	Thirsk	Flat	Turf	Afternoon

Notes

Saturday

05 August 2017

Doncaster	Flat	Turf	Afternoon
Goodwood	Flat	Turf	Afternoon
Hamilton Park	Flat	Turf	Evening
Lingfield Park	Flat	Turf	Evening
Newmarket	Flat	Turf	Afternoon
Thirsk	Flat	Turf	Afternoon

Notes

Sunday 06 August 2017	Chester	Flat	Turf	Afternoon
	Market Rasen	Jump	Turf	Afternoon

Notes

Monday 07 August 2017	Carlisle	Flat	Turf	Evening
	Ripon	Flat	Turf	Afternoon
	Salisbury	Flat	Turf	Afternoon
	Windsor	Flat	Turf	Evening

Notes

Tuesday	Catterick Bridge	Flat	Turf	Afternoon
08 August	Chelmsford City	Flat	AW	Evening
2017	Leicester	Flat	Turf	Afternoon
	Nottingham	Flat	Turf	Evening

Notes

Wednesday	Bath	Flat	Turf	Afternoon
09 August	Brighton	Flat	Turf	Afternoon
2017	Kempton Park	Flat	AW	Evening
	Pontefract	Flat	Turf	Afternoon
	Yarmouth	Flat	Turf	Evening

Notes

Thursday	Brighton	Flat	Turf	Afternoon
10 August	Haydock Park	Flat	Turf	Afternoon
2017	Newcastle	Flat	AW	Evening
	Sandown Park	Flat	Turf	Evening
	Wolves	Flat	AW	Evening
	Yarmouth	Flat	Turf	Afternoon

Notes

Friday	Brighton	Flat	Turf	Afternoon
11 August	Haydock Park	Flat	Turf	Evening
2017	Musselburgh	Flat	Turf	Afternoon
	Newmarket	Flat	Turf	Evening
	Wolves	Flat	AW	Afternoon

Notes

Saturday

12 August 2017

Ascot	Flat	Turf	Afternoon
Ayr	Flat	Turf	Evening
Haydock Park	Flat	Turf	Afternoon
Lingfield Park	Flat	Turf	Evening
Newmarket	Flat	Turf	Afternoon
Redcar	Flat	Turf	Afternoon

Notes

Sunday	Leicester	Flat	Turf	Afternoon
13 August 2017	Windsor	Flat	Turf	Afternoon

Notes

Monday	Ayr	Flat	Turf	Afternoon
14 August 2017	Ripon	Flat	Turf	Afternoon
	Windsor	Flat	Turf	Evening
	Wolves	Flat	AW	Evening

Notes

133

Tuesday	Chelmsford City	Flat	AW	Evening
15 August	Ffos Las	Flat	Turf	Afternoon
2017	Nottingham	Flat	Turf	Evening
	Thirsk	Flat	Turf	Afternoon

Notes

Wednesday	Bangor-On-Dee	Jump	Turf	Evening
16 August	Beverley	Flat	Turf	Afternoon
2017	Kempton Park	Flat	AW	Evening
	Newton Abbot	Jump	Turf	Afternoon
	Salisbury	Flat	Turf	Afternoon

Notes

Thursday	Beverley	Flat	Turf	Afternoon
17 August 2017	Chepstow	Flat	Turf	Evening
	Fontwell Park	Jump	Turf	Afternoon
	Salisbury	Flat	Turf	Afternoon
	Yarmouth	Flat	Turf	Evening
	Notes			

Friday	Catterick Bridge	Flat	Turf	Evening
18 August 2017	Newbury	Flat	Turf	Afternoon
	Newmarket	Flat	Turf	Evening
	Nottingham	Flat	Turf	Afternoon
	Wolves	Flat	AW	Afternoon
	Notes			

135

Saturday

19 August 2017

Bath	Flat	Turf	Evening
Doncaster	Flat	Turf	Afternoon
Market Rasen	Jump	Turf	Evening
Newbury	Flat	Turf	Afternoon
Newmarket	Flat	Turf	Afternoon
Perth	Jump	Turf	Afternoon
Ripon	Flat	Turf	Afternoon

Notes

Sunday	Pontefract	Flat	Turf	Afternoon
20 August 2017	Southwell	Jump	Turf	Afternoon

Notes

Monday	Hexham	Jump	Turf	Evening
21 August 2017	Lingfield Park	Flat	Turf	Afternoon
	Thirsk	Flat	Turf	Afternoon
	Windsor	Flat	Turf	Evening

Notes

137

Tuesday	Brighton	Flat	Turf	Afternoon
22 August 2017	Kempton Park	Flat	AW	Afternoon
	Newton Abbot	Jump	Turf	Evening
	Yarmouth	Flat	Turf	Evening

Notes

Wednesday	Bath	Flat	Turf	Afternoon
23 August 2017	Carlisle	Flat	Turf	Afternoon
	Kempton Park	Flat	AW	Evening
	Worcester	Jump	Turf	Evening
	York	Flat	Turf	Afternoon

Notes

THE JUDDMONTE INTERNATIONAL STAKES (CLASS 1)

138

Thursday	Chepstow	Flat	Turf	Afternoon
24 August	Fontwell Park	Jump	Turf	Evening
2017				
	Hamilton Park	Flat	Turf	Evening
	Stratford-On-Avon	Jump	Turf	Afternoon
	York	Flat	Turf	Afternoon

Notes

THE DARLEY YORKSHIRE OAKS (CLASS 1)
THE SKY BET LOWTHER STAKES (CLASS 1)

Friday	Ffos Las	Flat	Turf	Afternoon
25 August	Goodwood	Flat	Turf	Evening
2017				
	Hamilton Park	Flat	Turf	Evening
	Newmarket	Flat	Turf	Afternoon
	Salisbury	Flat	Turf	Evening
	York	Flat	Turf	Afternoon

Notes

THE COOLMORE NUNTHORPE STAKES (CLASS 1)

Saturday	Cartmel	Jump	Turf	Afternoon
26 August 2017	Chester	Flat	Turf	Afternoon
	Goodwood	Flat	Turf	Afternoon
	Newmarket	Flat	Turf	Afternoon
	Redcar	Flat	Turf	Evening
	Windsor	Flat	Turf	Evening
	York	Flat	Turf	Afternoon

Notes

THE WINTER HILL STAKES (CLASS 1)

THE IRISH THOROUGHBRED MARKETING GIMCRACK
STAKES (CLASS 1)
THE BETFRED STRENSALL STAKES

THE BETFRED EBOR (CLASS 2 HERITAGE HANDICAP)

Sunday 27 August 2017	Beverley	Flat	Turf	Afternoon
	Goodwood	Flat	Turf	Afternoon
	Yarmouth	Flat	Turf	Afternoon

Notes

Monday 28 August 2017 Summer bank holiday	Cartmel	Jump	Turf	Afternoon
	Chepstow	Flat	Turf	Afternoon
	Epsom Downs	Flat	Turf	Afternoon
	Ripon	Flat	Turf	Afternoon
	Southwell	Flat	AW	Afternoon

Notes

Tuesday	Carlisle	Flat	Turf	Evening
29 August	Epsom Downs	Flat	Turf	Afternoon
2017				
	Newton Abbot	Jump	Turf	Evening
	Ripon	Flat	Turf	Afternoon

Notes

Wednesday	Catterick Bridge	Flat	Turf	Afternoon
30 August	Kempton Park	Flat	AW	Evening
2017				
	Lingfield Park	Flat	Turf	Afternoon
	Musselburgh	Flat	Turf	Afternoon
	Worcester	Jump	Turf	Evening

Notes

Thursday	Bath	Flat	Turf	Afternoon
31 August 2017	Chelmsford City	Flat	AW	Afternoon
	Musselburgh	Flat	Turf	Afternoon
	Sedgefield	Jump	Turf	Evening
	Wolves	Flat	AW	Evening

Notes

Friday	Bangor-On-Dee	Jump	Turf	Afternoon
01 September 2017	Sandown Park	Flat	Turf	Afternoon
	Thirsk	Flat	Turf	Afternoon

Notes

143

Saturday

02
September
2017

Beverley	Flat	Turf	Afternoon
Chelmsford City	Flat	AW	Twilight
Chester	Flat	Turf	Afternoon
Hamilton Park	Flat	Turf	Twilight
Newton Abbot	Jump	Turf	Afternoon
Sandown Park	Flat	Turf	Afternoon

Notes

Sunday	Brighton	Flat	Turf	Afternoon
03 September 2017	Worcester	Jump	Turf	Afternoon

Notes

Monday	Brighton	Flat	Turf	Afternoon
04 September 2017	Ripon	Flat	Turf	Afternoon
	Windsor	Flat	Turf	Afternoon

Notes

Tuesday	Goodwood	Flat	Turf	Afternoon
05	Hamilton Park	Flat	Turf	Afternoon
September				
2017				
	Hexham	Jump	Turf	Afternoon
	Kempton Park	Flat	AW	Twilight

Notes

Wednesday	Chepstow	Flat	Turf	Afternoon
06	Kempton Park	Flat	AW	Twilight
September				
2017				
	Lingfield Park	Flat	Turf	Afternoon
	Southwell	Jump	Turf	Afternoon

Notes

Thursday 07 September 2017	Chelmsford City	Flat	AW	Evening
	Haydock Park	Flat	Turf	Afternoon
	Salisbury	Flat	Turf	Afternoon
	Sedgefield	Jump	Turf	Afternoon

Notes

Friday 08 September 2017	Ascot	Flat	Turf	Afternoon
	Haydock Park	Flat	Turf	Afternoon
	Kempton Park	Flat	AW	Evening
	Musselburgh	Flat	Turf	Evening
	Newcastle	Flat	AW	Afternoon

Notes

147

Saturday	Ascot	Flat	Turf	Afternoon
09 September 2017	Haydock Park	Flat	Turf	Afternoon
	Kempton Park	Flat	AW	Afternoon
	Stratford-On-Avon	Jump	Turf	Afternoon
	Thirsk	Flat	Turf	Afternoon
	Wolves	Flat	AW	Evening

Notes

THE BETFRED SPRINT CUP (CLASS 1)

148

Sunday	Fontwell Park	Jump	Turf	Afternoon
10 September 2017	York	Flat	Turf	Afternoon

Notes

Monday	Brighton	Flat	Turf	Afternoon
11 September 2017	Newton Abbot	Jump	Turf	Afternoon
	Perth	Jump	Turf	Afternoon

Notes

Tuesday	Catterick Bridge	Flat	Turf	Afternoon
12 September 2017	Leicester	Flat	Turf	Afternoon
	Newcastle	Flat	AW	Twilight
	Worcester	Jump	Turf	Afternoon

Notes

Wednesday	Carlisle	Flat	Turf	Afternoon
13 September 2017	Doncaster	Flat	Turf	Afternoon
	Kempton Park	Flat	AW	Twilight
	Uttoxeter	Jump	Turf	Afternoon

Notes

Thursday	Chepstow	Flat	Turf	Afternoon
14 September 2017	Doncaster	Flat	Turf	Afternoon
	Epsom Downs	Flat	Turf	Afternoon
	Hexham	Jump	Turf	Twilight

Notes

Friday	Chester	Flat	Turf	Afternoon
15 September 2017	Doncaster	Flat	Turf	Afternoon
	Salisbury	Flat	Turf	Twilight
	Sandown Park	Flat	Turf	Afternoon

Notes

151

Saturday	Bath	Flat	Turf	Afternoon
16 **September** **2017**	Chester	Flat	Turf	Afternoon
	Doncaster	Flat	Turf	Afternoon
	Lingfield Park	Flat	Turf	Afternoon
	Musselburgh	Flat	Turf	Twilight

Notes

THE SAINT GOBAIN WEBER PARK STAKES (CLASS 1)

THE AT THE RACES CHAMPAGNE STAKES (CLASS 1)

THE LADBROKES ST LEGER STAKES (CLASS 1)

Sunday	Bath	Flat	Turf	Afternoon
17 September 2017	Ffos Las	Flat	Turf	Afternoon

Notes

Monday	Brighton	Flat	Turf	Afternoon
18 September 2017	Carlisle	Flat	Turf	Afternoon
	Worcester	Jump	Turf	Afternoon

Notes

Tuesday	Chepstow	Flat	Turf	Afternoon
19	Newcastle	Flat	AW	Twilight
September				
2017				
	Redcar	Flat	Turf	Afternoon
	Yarmouth	Flat	Turf	Afternoon

Notes

Wednesday	Beverley	Flat	Turf	Afternoon
20	Kelso	Jump	Turf	Twilight
September				
2017				
	Sandown Park	Flat	Turf	Afternoon
	Yarmouth	Flat	Turf	Afternoon

Notes

Thursday	Ayr	Flat	Turf	Afternoon
21 September 2017	Chelmsford City	Flat	AW	Evening
	Pontefract	Flat	Turf	Afternoon
	Yarmouth	Flat	Turf	Afternoon

Notes

Friday	Ayr	Flat	Turf	Afternoon
22 September 2017	Newbury	Flat	Turf	Afternoon
	Newcastle	Flat	AW	Evening
	Newton Abbot	Jump	Turf	Afternoon

Notes

155

Ayr	Flat	Turf	Afternoon
Catterick Bridge	Flat	Turf	Afternoon
Newbury	Flat	Turf	Afternoon
Newmarket	Flat	Turf	Afternoon
Wolves	Flat	AW	Evening

Notes

THE WILLIAM HILL FIRTH OF CLYDE STAKES (CLASS 1)

THE WILLIAM HILL AYR GOLD CUP (HERITAGE
HANDICAP) (CLASS 2)
THE DUBAI DUTY FREE LEGACY CUP (CLASS 1)

THE DUBAI INTERNATIONAL AIRPORT WORLD TROPHY
(CLASS 1)
THE DUBAI DUTY FREE MILL REEF STAKES (CLASS 1)

Sunday	Plumpton	Jump	Turf	Afternoon
24 September 2017	Uttoxeter	Jump	Turf	Afternoon

Notes

Monday	Hamilton Park	Flat	Turf	Afternoon
25 September 2017	Kempton Park	Flat	AW	Afternoon
	Leicester	Flat	Turf	Afternoon

Notes

Tuesday	Beverley	Flat	Turf	Afternoon
26 September 2017	Chelmsford City	Flat	AW	Twilight
	Lingfield Park	Flat	AW	Afternoon
	Warwick	Jump	Turf	Afternoon

Notes

Wednesday	Goodwood	Flat	Turf	Afternoon
27 September 2017	Kempton Park	Flat	AW	Twilight
	Perth	Jump	Turf	Afternoon
	Redcar	Flat	Turf	Afternoon

Notes

Thursday 28 September 2017	Chelmsford City	Flat	AW	Evening
	Newmarket	Flat	Turf	Afternoon
	Perth	Jump	Turf	Afternoon
	Pontefract	Flat	Turf	Afternoon

Notes

Friday 29 September 2017	Haydock Park	Flat	Turf	Afternoon
	Newcastle	Flat	AW	Evening
	Newmarket	Flat	Turf	Afternoon
	Worcester	Jump	Turf	Afternoon

Notes

Saturday	Chelmsford City	Flat	AW	Twilight
30	Haydock Park	Flat	Turf	Afternoon
September				
2017				
	Market Rasen	Jump	Turf	Afternoon
	Newmarket	Flat	Turf	Afternoon
	Ripon	Flat	Turf	Afternoon

Notes

THE JUDDMONTE ROYAL LODGE STAKES (CLASS 1)

THE CONNOLLY'S RED MILLS CHEVELEY PARK STAKES

THE JUDDMONTE MIDDLE PARK STAKES (CLASS 1)

THE BETFRED CAMBRIDGESHIRE (CLASS 2 HERITAGE HANDICAP)

Sunday	Epsom Downs	Flat	Turf	Afternoon
01 October 2017	Musselburgh	Flat	Turf	Afternoon

Notes

Monday	Bath	Flat	Turf	Afternoon
02 October 2017	Newton Abbot	Jump	Turf	Afternoon
	Stratford-On-Avon	Jump	Turf	Afternoon

Notes

161

Tuesday	Ayr	Flat	Turf	Afternoon
03 October 2017	Kempton Park	Flat	AW	Twilight
	Sedgefield	Jump	Turf	Afternoon
	Southwell	Jump	Turf	Afternoon

Notes

Wednesday	Bangor-On-Dee	Jump	Turf	Afternoon
04 October 2017	Kempton Park	Flat	AW	Twilight
	Nottingham	Flat	Turf	Afternoon
	Salisbury	Flat	Turf	Afternoon

Notes

Thursday 05 October 2017	Chelmsford City	Flat	AW	Evening
	Huntingdon	Jump	Turf	Afternoon
	Lingfield Park	Flat	AW	Afternoon
	Warwick	Jump	Turf	Afternoon

Notes

Friday 06 October 2017	Ascot	Flat	Turf	Afternoon
	Chelmsford City	Flat	AW	Evening
	Fontwell Park	Jump	Turf	Afternoon
	Hexham	Jump	Turf	Afternoon

Notes

163

Saturday

07 October 2017

Ascot	Flat	Turf	Afternoon
Chester	Flat	Turf	Afternoon
Fontwell Park	Jump	Turf	Afternoon
Newmarket	Flat	Turf	Afternoon
Redcar	Flat	Turf	Afternoon
Wolves	Flat	AW	Evening

Notes

Sunday	Kelso	Jump	Turf	Afternoon
08 October 2017	Uttoxeter	Jump	Turf	Afternoon

Notes

Monday	Pontefract	Flat	Turf	Afternoon
09 October 2017	Salisbury	Flat	Turf	Afternoon
	Windsor	Flat	Turf	Afternoon

Notes

Tuesday 10 October 2017

Brighton	Flat	Turf	Afternoon
Catterick Bridge	Flat	Turf	Afternoon
Leicester	Flat	Turf	Afternoon
Newcastle	Flat	AW	Twilight

Notes

Wednesday 11 October 2017

Kempton Park	Flat	AW	Twilight
Ludlow	Jump	Turf	Afternoon
Nottingham	Flat	Turf	Afternoon
Towcester	Jump	Turf	Afternoon

Notes

Thursday	Ayr	Flat	Turf	Afternoon
12 October 2017	Chelmsford City	Flat	AW	Evening
	Exeter	Jump	Turf	Afternoon
	Worcester	Jump	Turf	Afternoon

Notes

Friday	Kempton Park	Flat	AW	Evening
13 October 2017	Newmarket	Flat	Turf	Afternoon
	Newton Abbot	Jump	Turf	Afternoon
	York	Flat	Turf	Afternoon

Notes

167

Saturday	Chepstow	Jump	Turf	Afternoon
14 October 2017	Hexham	Jump	Turf	Afternoon
	Kempton Park	Flat	AW	Twilight
	Newmarket	Flat	Turf	Afternoon
	York	Flat	Turf	Afternoon

Notes

THE totepool SILVER TROPHY HANDICAP HURDLE RACE

THE DUBAI DEWHURST STAKES (CLASS 1)

THE DARLEY STAKES (CLASS 1)

THE VISION AUTUMN STAKES (CLASS 1)

THE BETFRED CESAREWITCH (HERITAGE HANDICAP) (CLASS 2)

Sunday	Chepstow	Jump	Turf	Afternoon
15 October 2017	Goodwood	Flat	Turf	Afternoon

Notes

Monday	Musselburgh	Flat	Turf	Afternoon
16 October 2017	Windsor	Flat	Turf	Afternoon
	Yarmouth	Flat	Turf	Afternoon

Notes

Tuesday	Hereford	Jump	Turf	Afternoon
17 October 2017	Huntingdon	Jump	Turf	Afternoon
	Kempton Park	Flat	AW	Twilight
	Leicester	Flat	Turf	Afternoon

Notes

Wednesday	Bath	Flat	Turf	Afternoon
18 October 2017	Kempton Park	Flat	AW	Twilight
	Nottingham	Flat	Turf	Afternoon
	Wetherby	Jump	Turf	Afternoon

Notes

Thursday	Brighton	Flat	Turf	Afternoon
19 October	Carlisle	Jump	Turf	Afternoon
2017				
	Newcastle	Flat	AW	Evening
	Uttoxeter	Jump	Turf	Afternoon

Notes

Friday	Fakenham	Jump	Turf	Afternoon
20 October	Haydock Park	Flat	Turf	Afternoon
2017				
	Newcastle	Flat	AW	Evening
	Redcar	Flat	Turf	Afternoon
	Wincanton	Jump	Turf	Afternoon

Notes

Saturday	Ascot	Flat	Turf	Afternoon
21 October	Catterick Bridge	Flat	Turf	Afternoon
2017	Ffos Las	Jump	Turf	Afternoon
	Market Rasen	Jump	Turf	Afternoon
	Stratford-On-Avon	Jump	Turf	Afternoon
	Wolves	Flat	AW	Evening

Notes

THE QUEEN ELIZABETH II STAKES SPONSORED BY QIPCO (CLASS 1)

THE QIPCO BRITISH CHAMPIONS SPRINT STAKES (CLASS 1)

THE QIPCO BRITISH CHAMPIONS LONG DISTANCE CUP (CLASS 1)

THE QIPCO CHAMPION STAKES (CLASS 1)

THE QIPCO BRITISH CHAMPIONS FILLIES & MARES STAKES (CLASS 1)

Sunday	Kempton Park	Jump	Turf	Afternoon
22 October	Southwell	Flat	AW	Afternoon
2017				

Notes

Monday	Plumpton	Jump	Turf	Afternoon
23 October	Pontefract	Flat	Turf	Afternoon
2017	Windsor	Flat	Turf	Afternoon

Notes

Tuesday	Exeter	Jump	Turf	Afternoon
24 October	Kempton Park	Flat	AW	Twilight
2017				
	Newcastle	Flat	AW	Afternoon
	Yarmouth	Flat	Turf	Afternoon

Notes

Wednesday	Kempton Park	Flat	AW	Twilight
25 October	Newmarket	Flat	Turf	Afternoon
2017				
	Sedgefield	Jump	Turf	Afternoon
	Worcester	Jump	Turf	Afternoon

Notes

Thursday	Carlisle	Jump	Turf	Afternoon
26 October	Chelmsford City	Flat	AW	Evening
2017	Ludlow	Jump	Turf	Afternoon
	Southwell	Jump	Turf	Afternoon

Notes

Friday	Cheltenham	Jump	Turf	Afternoon
27 October	Doncaster	Flat	Turf	Afternoon
2017	Newbury	Flat	Turf	Afternoon
	Wolves	Flat	AW	Evening

Notes

175

Saturday	Cheltenham	Jump	Turf	Afternoon
28 October 2017	Doncaster	Flat	Turf	Afternoon
	Kelso	Jump	Turf	Afternoon
	Newbury	Flat	Turf	Afternoon
	Wolves	Flat	AW	Twilight

Notes

THE RACING POST TROPHY (CLASS 1)

THE HORRIS HILL STAKES (CLASS 1)

THE ST SIMON STAKES (CLASS 1)

Sunday	Aintree	Jump	Turf	Afternoon
29 October	Wincanton	Jump	Turf	Afternoon
2017				

Notes

Monday	Ayr	Jump	Turf	Afternoon
30 October	Leicester	Flat	Turf	Afternoon
2017	Redcar	Flat	Turf	Afternoon

Notes

Tuesday 31 October 2017	Bangor-On-Dee	Jump	Turf	Afternoon
	Catterick Bridge	Flat	Turf	Afternoon
	Chepstow	Jump	Turf	Afternoon
	Wolves	Flat	AW	Twilight

Notes

Wednesday 01 November 2017	Fakenham	Jump	Turf	Afternoon
	Kempton Park	Flat	AW	Twilight
	Nottingham	Flat	Turf	Afternoon
	Taunton	Jump	Turf	Afternoon

Notes

Thursday 02 November 2017	Chelmsford City	Flat	AW	Evening
	Lingfield Park	Flat	AW	Afternoon
	Sedgefield	Jump	Turf	Afternoon
	Stratford-On-Avon	Jump	Turf	Afternoon

Notes

Friday 03 November 2017	Newcastle	Flat	AW	Evening
	Newmarket	Flat	Turf	Afternoon
	Uttoxeter	Jump	Turf	Afternoon
	Wetherby	Jump	Turf	Afternoon

Notes

Saturday	Ascot	Jump	Turf	Afternoon
04 **November** **2017**	Ayr	Jump	Turf	Afternoon
	Newcastle	Flat	AW	Twilight
	Newmarket	Flat	Turf	Afternoon
	Wetherby	Jump	Turf	Afternoon

Notes

| Sunday | Carlisle | Jump | Turf | Afternoon |
| **05** **November** **2017** | Huntingdon | Jump | Turf | Afternoon |

Notes

Monday	Kempton Park	Flat	AW	Afternoon
06 **November** **2017**	Plumpton	Jump	Turf	Afternoon
	Southwell	Jump	Turf	Afternoon

Notes

Tuesday	Exeter	Jump	Turf	Afternoon
07 November 2017	Kempton Park	Flat	AW	Twilight
	Redcar	Flat	Turf	Afternoon
	Wolves	Flat	AW	Afternoon

Notes

Wednesday	Chepstow	Jump	Turf	Afternoon
08 November 2017	Kempton Park	Flat	AW	Twilight
	Musselburgh	Jump	Turf	Afternoon
	Nottingham	Flat	Turf	Afternoon

Notes

Thursday	Chelmsford City	Flat	AW	Evening
09	Ludlow	Jump	Turf	Afternoon
November				
2017				
	Market Rasen	Jump	Turf	Afternoon
	Newbury	Jump	Turf	Afternoon

Notes

Friday	Fontwell Park	Jump	Turf	Afternoon
10	Hexham	Jump	Turf	Afternoon
November				
2017				
	Newcastle	Flat	AW	Evening
	Warwick	Jump	Turf	Afternoon

Notes

Saturday

11
November
2017

Aintree	Jump	Turf	Afternoon
Doncaster	Flat	Turf	Afternoon
Kelso	Jump	Turf	Afternoon
Wincanton	Jump	Turf	Afternoon
Wolves	Flat	AW	Twilight

Notes

Sunday	Ffos Las	Jump	Turf	Afternoon
12 **November** **2017**	Sandown Park	Jump	Turf	Afternoon

Notes

Monday	Carlisle	Jump	Turf	Afternoon
13 **November** **2017**	Kempton Park	Jump	Turf	Afternoon
	Southwell	Flat	AW	Afternoon

Notes

Tuesday	Hereford	Jump	Turf	Afternoon
14	Huntingdon	Jump	Turf	Afternoon
November				
2017	Lingfield Park	Jump	Turf	Afternoon

Notes

Wednesday	Ayr	Jump	Turf	Afternoon
15	Bangor-On-Dee	Jump	Turf	Afternoon
November				
2017	Exeter	Jump	Turf	Afternoon
	Newcastle	Flat	AW	Twilight

Notes

Thursday	Chelmsford City	Flat	AW	Evening
16 November 2017	Ludlow	Jump	Turf	Afternoon
	Southwell	Flat	AW	Afternoon
	Taunton	Jump	Turf	Afternoon

Notes

Friday	Chelmsford City	Flat	AW	Evening
17 November 2017	Cheltenham	Jump	Turf	Afternoon
	Lingfield Park	Flat	AW	Afternoon
	Newcastle	Jump	Turf	Afternoon

Notes

Saturday	Cheltenham	Jump	Turf	Afternoon
18	Lingfield Park	Flat	AW	Afternoon
November				
2017				
	Uttoxeter	Jump	Turf	Afternoon
	Wetherby	Jump	Turf	Afternoon
	Wolves	Flat	AW	Evening

Notes

Sunday	Cheltenham	Jump	Turf	Afternoon
19 November 2017	Fontwell Park	Jump	Turf	Afternoon

Notes

Monday	Leicester	Jump	Turf	Afternoon
20 November 2017	Plumpton	Jump	Turf	Afternoon
	Wolves	Flat	AW	Afternoon

Notes

Tuesday	Fakenham	Jump	Turf	Afternoon
21	Lingfield Park	Flat	AW	Afternoon
November				
2017				
	Southwell	Jump	Turf	Afternoon

Notes

Wednesday	Chepstow	Jump	Turf	Afternoon
22	Hexham	Jump	Turf	Afternoon
November				
2017				
	Kempton Park	Flat	AW	Twilight
	Warwick	Jump	Turf	Afternoon

Notes

Thursday	Chelmsford City	Flat	AW	Evening
23	Market Rasen	Jump	Turf	Afternoon
November				
2017	Newcastle	Flat	AW	Afternoon
	Wincanton	Jump	Turf	Afternoon

Notes

Friday	Ascot	Jump	Turf	Afternoon
24	Catterick Bridge	Jump	Turf	Afternoon
November				
2017	Ffos Las	Jump	Turf	Afternoon
	Newcastle	Flat	AW	Evening

Notes

Saturday

25
November
2017

Ascot	Jump	Turf	Afternoon
Haydock Park	Jump	Turf	Afternoon
Huntingdon	Jump	Turf	Afternoon
Lingfield Park	Flat	AW	Afternoon
Wolves	Flat	AW	Evening

Notes

192

Sunday	Exeter	Jump	Turf	Afternoon
26 November 2017	Uttoxeter	Jump	Turf	Afternoon

Notes

Monday	Ayr	Jump	Turf	Afternoon
27 November 2017	Kempton Park	Jump	Turf	Afternoon
	Ludlow	Jump	Turf	Afternoon

Notes

Tuesday 28 November 2017

Lingfield Park	Jump	Turf	Afternoon
Sedgefield	Jump	Turf	Afternoon
Southwell	Flat	AW	Afternoon

Notes

Wednesday 29 November 2017

Hereford	Jump	Turf	Afternoon
Kempton Park	Flat	AW	Twilight
Wetherby	Jump	Turf	Afternoon
Wolves	Flat	AW	Afternoon

Notes

Thursday	Musselburgh	Jump	Turf	Afternoon
30 November 2017	Newcastle	Flat	AW	Evening
	Taunton	Jump	Turf	Afternoon
St Andrew's Day (Scotland)	Towcester	Jump	Turf	Afternoon

Notes

Friday	Chelmsford City	Flat	AW	Evening
01 December 2017	Doncaster	Jump	Turf	Afternoon
	Newbury	Jump	Turf	Afternoon
	Southwell	Flat	AW	Afternoon

Notes

Saturday	Bangor-On-Dee	Jump	Turf	Afternoon
02	Doncaster	Jump	Turf	Afternoon
December				
2017				
	Newbury	Jump	Turf	Afternoon
	Newcastle	Jump	Turf	Afternoon
	Wolves	Flat	AW	Evening

Notes

THE HENNESSY GOLD CUP STEEPLE CHASE (HANDICAP)

THE RSA WORCESTER NOVICES' STEEPLE CHASE (CLASS 1)

THE StanJames.com FIGHTING FIFTH HURDLE RACE (CLASS 1)

| **Sunday** | Carlisle | Jump | Turf | Afternoon |
| **03 December 2017** | Leicester | Jump | Turf | Afternoon |

Notes

Monday	Fakenham	Jump	Turf	Afternoon
04 December 2017	Plumpton	Jump	Turf	Afternoon
	Southwell	Flat	AW	Afternoon

Notes

Tuesday	Lingfield Park	Jump	Turf	Afternoon
05	Southwell	Jump	Turf	Afternoon
December				
2017				
	Wolves	Flat	AW	Afternoon

Notes

Wednesday	Haydock Park	Jump	Turf	Afternoon
06	Lingfield Park	Flat	AW	Afternoon
December				
2017				
	Ludlow	Jump	Turf	Afternoon
	Newcastle	Flat	AW	Twilight

Notes

Thursday

07
December
2017

Chelmsford City	Flat	AW	Evening
Leicester	Jump	Turf	Afternoon
Market Rasen	Jump	Turf	Afternoon
Wincanton	Jump	Turf	Afternoon

Notes

Friday

08
December
2017

Chelmsford City	Flat	AW	Evening
Exeter	Jump	Turf	Afternoon
Sandown Park	Jump	Turf	Afternoon
Sedgefield	Jump	Turf	Afternoon

Notes

Saturday	Aintree	Jump	Turf	Afternoon
09	Chepstow	Jump	Turf	Afternoon
December				
2017				
	Sandown Park	Jump	Turf	Afternoon
	Wetherby	Jump	Turf	Afternoon
	Wolves	Flat	AW	Evening

Notes

THE BETFRED BECHER HANDICAP STEEPLE CHASE (CLASS 1)

THE BETFAIR TINGLE CREEK STEEPLE CHASE (CLASS 1)

THE RACING POST HENRY VIII NOVICES' STEEPLE CHASE (CLASS 1)

Sunday	Huntingdon	Jump	Turf	Afternoon
10 December 2017	Kelso	Jump	Turf	Afternoon

Notes

Monday	Fontwell Park	Jump	Turf	Afternoon
11 December 2017	Musselburgh	Jump	Turf	Afternoon
	Southwell	Flat	AW	Afternoon

Notes

Tuesday	Ayr	Jump	Turf	Afternoon
12	Lingfield Park	Flat	AW	Afternoon
December				
2017				
	Uttoxeter	Jump	Turf	Afternoon

Notes

Wednesday	Hexham	Jump	Turf	Afternoon
13	Kempton Park	Flat	AW	Twilight
December				
2017				
	Leicester	Jump	Turf	Afternoon
	Lingfield Park	Flat	AW	Afternoon

Notes

Thursday	Chelmsford City	Flat	AW	Evening
14	Newcastle	Jump	Turf	Afternoon
December				
2017	Taunton	Jump	Turf	Afternoon
	Warwick	Jump	Turf	Afternoon

Notes

Friday	Bangor-On-Dee	Jump	Turf	Afternoon
15	Chelmsford City	Flat	AW	Evening
December				
2017	Cheltenham	Jump	Turf	Afternoon
	Doncaster	Jump	Turf	Afternoon

Notes

Saturday

16
December
2017

Cheltenham	Jump	Turf	Afternoon
Doncaster	Jump	Turf	Afternoon
Hereford	Jump	Turf	Afternoon
Newcastle	Flat	AW	Afternoon
Wolves	Flat	AW	Evening

Notes

Sunday	Carlisle	Jump	Turf	Afternoon
17 December 2017	Southwell	Jump	Turf	Afternoon

Notes

Monday	Ffos Las	Jump	Turf	Afternoon
18 December 2017	Plumpton	Jump	Turf	Afternoon
	Wolves	Flat	AW	Afternoon

Notes

Tuesday	Catterick Bridge	Jump	Turf	Afternoon
19	Fakenham	Jump	Turf	Afternoon
December				
2017				
	Southwell	Flat	AW	Afternoon

Notes

Wednesday	Kempton Park	Flat	AW	Twilight
20	Lingfield Park	Flat	AW	Afternoon
December				
2017				
	Ludlow	Jump	Turf	Afternoon
	Newbury	Jump	Turf	Afternoon

Notes

Thursday	Chelmsford City	Flat	AW	Evening
21 December 2017	Exeter	Jump	Turf	Afternoon
	Southwell	Flat	AW	Afternoon
	Towcester	Jump	Turf	Afternoon

Notes

Friday	Ascot	Jump	Turf	Afternoon
22 December 2017	Southwell	Flat	AW	Afternoon
	Uttoxeter	Jump	Turf	Afternoon
	Wolves	Flat	AW	Evening

Notes

Saturday

23
December
2017

Ascot	Jump	Turf	Afternoon
Haydock Park	Jump	Turf	Afternoon
Lingfield Park	Flat	AW	Afternoon
Newcastle	Jump	Turf	Afternoon

Notes

Sunday

24
December
2017

Notes

Monday

25
December
2017

Christmas
Day

Notes

Tuesday	Fontwell Park	Jump	Turf	Afternoon
26	Huntingdon	Jump	Turf	Afternoon
December				
2017				
	Kempton Park	Jump	Turf	Afternoon
Boxing Day	Market Rasen	Jump	Turf	Afternoon
	Sedgefield	Jump	Turf	Afternoon
	Wetherby	Jump	Turf	Afternoon
	Wincanton	Jump	Turf	Afternoon
	Wolves	Flat	AW	Afternoon

Notes

THE KAUTO STAR NOVICES' STEEPLE CHASE (CLASS 1)

THE CHRISTMAS HURDLE RACE (CLASS 1)

THE KING GEORGE VI STEEPLE CHASE (CLASS 1)

THE 188BET ROWLAND MEYRICK HANDICAP STEEPLE CHASE

Wednesday	Chepstow	Jump	Turf	Afternoon
27	Kempton Park	Jump	Turf	Afternoon
December				
2017	Wetherby	Jump	Turf	Afternoon
	Wolves	Flat	AW	Afternoon

Notes

THE coral.co.uk FUTURE CHAMPIONS FINALE JUVENILE
HURDLE RACE
THE CORAL WELSH GRAND NATIONAL (A HANDICAP
STEEPLE CHASE)
THE WAYWARD LAD NOVICES' STEEPLE CHASE (CLASS 1)

THE DESERT ORCHID STEEPLE CHASE (CLASS 1)

Thursday	Catterick Bridge	Jump	Turf	Afternoon
28	Leicester	Jump	Turf	Afternoon
December				
2017	Lingfield Park	Flat	AW	Afternoon

Notes

211

Friday	Doncaster	Jump	Turf	Afternoon
29	Kelso	Jump	Turf	Afternoon
December				
2017	Southwell	Flat	AW	Afternoon

Notes

Saturday	Haydock Park	Jump	Turf	Afternoon
30	Lingfield Park	Flat	AW	Afternoon
December				
2017	Newbury	Jump	Turf	Afternoon
	Taunton	Jump	Turf	Afternoon

Notes

Sunday

31 December 2017

Lingfield Park	Flat	AW	Afternoon
Uttoxeter	Jump	Turf	Afternoon
Warwick	Jump	Turf	Afternoon

Notes

2018

213

2017 Yearly Planner

2017	Jan	Feb	Mar	Apr	May	Jun	Jul	Aug	Sep	Oct	Nov	Dec
M					1							
T					2		1					
W		1	1		3			2			1	
T		2	2		4	1		3			2	
F		3	3		5	2		4	1		3	1
S		4	4	1	6	3	1	5	2		4	2
S	1	5	5	2	7	4	2	6	3	1	5	3
M	2	6	6	3	8	5	3	7	4	2	6	4
T	3	7	7	4	9	6	4	8	5	3	7	5
W	4	8	8	5	10	7	5	9	6	4	8	6
T	5	9	9	6	11	8	6	10	7	5	9	7
F	6	10	10	7	12	9	7	11	8	6	10	8
S	7	11	11	8	13	10	8	12	9	7	11	9
S	8	12	12	9	14	11	9	13	10	8	12	10
M	9	13	13	10	15	12	10	14	11	9	13	11
T	10	14	14	11	16	13	11	15	12	10	14	12
W	11	15	15	12	17	14	12	16	13	11	15	13
T	12	16	16	13	18	15	13	17	14	12	16	14
F	13	17	17	14	19	16	14	18	15	13	17	15
S	14	18	18	15	20	17	15	19	16	14	18	16
S	15	19	19	16	21	18	16	20	17	15	19	17
M	16	20	20	17	22	19	17	21	18	16	20	18
T	17	21	21	18	23	20	18	22	19	17	21	19
W	18	22	22	19	24	21	19	23	20	18	22	20
T	19	23	23	20	25	22	20	24	21	19	23	21
F	20	24	24	21	26	23	21	25	22	20	24	22
S	21	25	25	22	27	24	22	26	23	21	25	23
S	22	26	26	23	28	25	23	27	24	22	26	24
M	23	27	27	24	29	26	24	28	25	23	27	25
T	24	28	28	25	30	27	25	29	26	24	28	26
W	25		29	26	31	28	26	30	27	25	29	27
T	26		30	27		29	27	31	28	26	30	28
F	27		31	28		30	28		29	27		29
S	28			29			29		30	28		30
S	29			30			30			29		31
M	30						31			30		
T	31									31		

214

www.ingramcontent.com/pod-product-compliance
Lightning Source LLC
Chambersburg PA
CBHW060500290526
45791CB00001B/198